D1152357

THE WEST HAM
UNITED QUIZ BOOK

THE WEST HAM UNITED QUIZ BOOK

Compiled by Chris Cowlin

Foreword by Julian Dicks

APEX PUBLISHING LTD

Paperback first published in 2006, Reprinted and Updated in 2007, 2008 and 2009, Hardback first published in 2008, Reprinted and Updated in 2009 by

Apex Publishing Ltd
PO Box 7086, Clacton on Sea, Essex, CO15 5WN, England
www.apexpublishing.co.uk

Copyright © 2006-2008 by Chris Cowlin
The author has asserted his moral rights

British Library Cataloguing-in-Publication Data
A catalogue record for this book
is available from the British Library

ISBN PAPERBACK: 1-904444-99-7   978-1904444-99-2
ISBN HARDBACK: 1-906358-23-0   978-1906358-23-5

All rights reserved. This book is sold subject to the condition, that no part of this book is to be reproduced, in any shape or form. Or by way of trade, stored in a retrieval system or transmitted in any form or by any means, electronic, mechanical, photocopying, recording, be lent, re-sold, hired out or otherwise circulated in any form of binding or cover other than that in which it is published and without a similar condition, including this condition being imposed on the subsequent purchaser, without prior permission of the copyright holder.

Typeset in 10.5pt Chianti Bdlt Win95BT
Printed in Great Britain by the MPG Books Group,
Bodmin and King's Lynn

Cover Design: Siobhan Smith

Author's Note:
Please can you contact me: ChrisCowlin@btconnect.com if you find any mistakes/errors in this book as I would like to put them right on any future reprints of this book. I would also like to hear from West Ham fans who have enjoyed the test! For more information on me and my books please look at: www.ChrisCowlin.com

This book is in no way officially associated with West Ham United Football Club.

I would like to dedicate this book to:

Julia, for being a great wife,
Harry - my fantastic son,
and to Hayley, my helpful and loving sister.

FOREWORD

When I joined West Ham United, I didn't know what to expect. John Lyall sold the club to me saying how great it was and how great the supporters are. I remember my first game against Everton and elbowing Trevor Steven - I didn't mean it (honest). I knew I would have a great reputation with the West Ham supporters. In my 11 years at West Ham I can honestly say I enjoyed all of them, but the one game that stands out is when we beat Cambridge at home on the final day winning 2-1, and I set up the winning goal for Clive Allen, and getting promotion - that was a great day. West Ham has always had great players, but the ones that stand out for me are Liam Brady, Billy Bonds, Alan Devonshire, Phil Parkes, Alvin Martin, Frank McAvennie and Tony Cottee. However, if I had to choose one it would be Liam Brady - he was truly magnificent! I was also privileged to play with the younger generation, which includes Rio Ferdinand, Joe Cole and Frank Lampard.This book is a must for all West Ham United supporters. It will test your knowledge of West Ham players, past and present, and the history of this great club. I would like to thank everyone at West Ham, especially the supporters, for my enjoyable 11 years, and I hope you have great fun with this book.

Julian Dicks

INTRODUCTION

I would first of all like to thank Julian Dicks for writing the foreword to this book. Julian was a true legend for the Hammers and I am very grateful for his help on this project.

I would also like to thank all the past legends of West Ham United Football Club and many current employees of the club for their comments and reviews on this book (these can be found at the back of the book).

I am honoured to donate £1 from each book sale to 'The Willow Foundation Charity'. It is a registered charity - **www.willowfoundation.org.uk** dedicated to improving the quality of life of seriously ill young adults aged 16 to 40 throughout the UK, by organising and funding a 'Special Day' of their choice. I would like to thank the Chief Executive of The Willow Foundation, David Williams, for his support in creating this book.

I would also like to thank Peter Stewart for his help and advice during the books compilation.

I hope you enjoy this book. Hopefully it should bring back some wonderful memories!

In closing, I would like to thank all my friends and family for encouraging me to complete this book.

Chris Cowlin.

Best wishes
Chris Cowlin

www.apexpublishing.co.uk

BOBBY MOORE

1.   In which year was Bobby born?

2.   When Bobby lifted the World Cup trophy in 1966, what
      other two West Ham players did the same that day?

3.   How many England caps did Bobby win?

4.   In what year did Bobby sign for West Ham - 1956,
      1957 or 1958?

5.   1975 marked Bobby's final Wembley appearance in an
      FA Cup final, and the team lost 2-0, against who?

6.   In 1958 Bobby made his West Ham debut in a 3-2
      home win, against who?

7.   How old was Bobby when he made his West Ham
      debut?

8.   In 1974 who did Bobby sign for from West Ham?

9.   In what year was his last England cap and 90th as
      captain?

10.   In 1984 Bobby was appointed manager of who?

TREVOR BROOKING

11. In what year was Trevor born - 1943, 1946 or 1948?

12. Trevor made his West Ham debut in 1967, against who?

13. How many times did Trevor win "Hammer of the Year" - 3, 4 or 5?

14. Trevor scored in the 1980 FA Cup final. Who did West Ham play?

15. What was Trevor's nickname at the Hammers?

16. How many League appearances has Trevor made for West Ham - 524, 526 or 528?

17. Trevor's last game for West Ham was against Everton, in what year?

18. How many caps did Trevor win for England - 46, 47 or 48?

19. How many goals did he score for England - 4, 5 or 6?

20. Against which country did Trevor make his full England debut?

WEST HAM IN THE LEAGUE CUP

21. Which two players both scored hat-tricks in a 7-0 win against Leeds United in November 1966?

22. Which team knocked West Ham out of the competition in the quarter-finals in the 1982-1983 season?

23. Can you name the two London clubs that West Ham knocked out on their way to the 1981 Cup final?

24. What West Ham midfielder scored a hat-trick in a 4-1 win over Walsall in November 1997?

25. In the 1983-1984 season West Ham won 10-0 in their 2nd round, 2nd leg tie. Who were the opponents?

26. Which player scored five League goals during the 1979-1980 season?

27. Which two Midlands sides did West Ham beat in the 3rd and 4th rounds during the 1997-1998 season?

28. Which two Midlands clubs did West Ham knock out on their way in the 1989-1990 Cup run?

29. Tony Cottee scored a hat-trick in the League Cup in October 1986. Who were the opponents?

30. Which player scored four goals in a 4-1 win over Bolton Wanderers in October 1967?

SQUAD NUMBERS 2009-2010

Match the player with his squad number for the 2009-2010 season

31.	Kieron Dyer	15
32.	Mark Noble	34
33.	Carlton Cole	31
34.	Scott Parker	14
35.	Oliver Lee	7
36.	Jack Collison	17
37.	Matthew Upson	12
38.	Robert Green	8
39.	Luis Jimenez	16
40.	Radoslav Kovac	1

PLAYER OF THE YEAR

Match the player with the season in which he became Player of the Year

41.   2003-2004   *Julian Dicks*

42.   2001-2002   *Trevor Morley*

43.   1999-2000   *Rio Ferdinand*

44.   1997-1998   *Paolo Di Canio*

45.   1995-1996   *Matthew Etherington*

46.   1993-1994   *Sebastien Schemmel*

47.   1991-1992   *Stewart Robson*

48.   1989-1990   *Tony Cottee*

49.   1987-1988   *Julian Dicks*

50.   1985-1986   *Julian Dicks*

POSITIONS IN THE LEAGUE

Match the League position with the season in which it was achieved

51.	2005-2006	15th in the Premier League
52.	2001-2002	10th in the Premier League
53.	2000-2001	9th in the Premier League
54.	1995-1996	7th in the Premier League
55.	1991-1992	7th in Division Two
56.	1987-1988	12th in Division One
57.	1981-1982	6th in Division One
58.	1979-1980	22nd in Division One
59.	1972-1973	9th in Division One
60.	1965-1966	16th in Division One

JULIAN DICKS

61. In which year was Julian born - 1967, 1968 or 1969?

62. Where did West Ham sign Julian from (1st spell)?

63. How many England under-21 caps did Julian win?

64. Julian made his Hammers debut in 1988 in a 2-0 defeat, against who?

65. What was Julian's nickname at West Ham?

66. Which manager signed Julian for West Ham (1st spell)?

67. How many times did Julian win 'Hammer of the Year' - 2, 3 or 4?

68. Which team did West Ham play in Julian's benefit match in 2000?

69. When Julian moved to Liverpool from West Ham, which two players moved in the other direction?

70. In 1993, Julian was playing for Liverpool and was the last person to score in front of the standing Kop. Who was the game against?

ALAN DEVONSHIRE

71. In what year was Alan born - 1954, 1956 or 1958?

72. Against which club did Alan make his West Ham debut?

73. When Alan left West Ham, who did he join?

74. Can you name the season in which Alan won "Hammer of the Year"?

75. Against which two clubs did Alan score his first three goals for West Ham?

76. Which manager signed Alan for West Ham?

77. How much did Alan cost West Ham in 1976?

78. Who did Alan score against in the 1980 FA Cup semi-final replay in a 2-1 win?

79. Alan made his England debut in a 1-1 draw in May 1980, against who?

80. How many England caps did Alan win - 6, 8 or 10?

TONY COTTEE

81. How many times did Tony play for England - 6, 7 or 8?

82. In what year was Tony born - 1964, 1965 or 1966?

83. In what year did Tony win the PFA Young Player of the Year award?

84. What is Tony's nickname?

85. Can you name the Malaysian side that Tony played for during his career?

86. When Tony signed for Everton in 1988, how much was it for?

87. Tony made his West Ham debut in 1983, against who?

88. Who did Tony make his England debut against?

89. How many goals did Tony score in his first season at Upton Park during the 1982-1983 season?

90. Which other London side has Tony played for, making two appearances?

TOMMY TAYLOR

91. In what year was Tommy born?

92. Where did West Ham sign Tommy from?

93. When the Hammers signed Tommy, what player went in the other direction as part of the deal?

94. How many England under-23 caps did Tommy win - 11, 12 or 13?

95. How many League appearances did Tommy make for West Ham - 240, 340 or 440?

96. Tommy made 30 League appearances in his first season at Upton Park, scoring one goal, against who?

97. Tommy appeared in all 42 League games during the 1971-1972 season. What other three West Ham players have done the same?

98. What London club did Tommy score against during the 1972-1973 season in both the home and away games?

99. How many League goals did Tommy score in his West Ham career - 6, 7 or 8?

100. When Tommy left West Ham in 1979, who did he join?

MANAGER: GIANFRANCO ZOLA

101. In which year was Gianfranco born in Oliena, Sardinia – 1964, 1965 or 1966?

102. How many goals did Gianfranco score for Italy in his 35 international appearances?

103. Which defender did Gianfranco sign for The Hammers from Fiorentina in August 2009?

104. In which year did Gianfranco take over as West Ham manager?

105. In which position did Gianfranco guide West Ham during his first season in charge at Upton Park – 9th, 11th or 13th?

106. Against which team did Gianfranco record his first West Ham United win as manager, a 1-0 away win with Valon Behrami scoring the only goal for The Hammers?

107. Which manager did Gianfranco take over from when he arrived at Upton Park?

108. True or false: Gianfranco's appointment as West Ham manager was his first managerial role in England?

109. For which Premier League team did Gianfranco play between 1996 and 2003?

110. Which Spanish forward did Gianfranco sign for The Hammers

POSITIONS IN THE LEAGUE

Match the League position with the season in which it was achieved

111.	*2002-2003*	*14th in the Premier League*
112.	*1997-1998*	*12th in Division Two*
113.	*1996-1997*	*18th in Division One*
114.	*1993-1994*	*8th in Division One*
115.	*1988-1989*	*18th in the Premier League*
116.	*1984-1985*	*20th in Division One*
117.	*1977-1978*	*16th in Division One*
118.	*1975-1976*	*19th in Division One*
119.	*1968-1969*	*13th in the Premier League*
120.	*1951-1952*	*8th in the Premier League*

2008-2009

121. Which striker scored a brace for The Hammers in a 4-1 away win against Portsmouth on Boxing Day 2008?

122. Which team did West Ham beat 2-1 at home on the opening day of the League season with Dean Ashton scoring both goals?

123. How many of West Ham's 38 League games did the club win – 10, 12 or 14?

124. Which Spanish forward scored West Ham's only goal in the 1-0 away win against Stoke City during May 2009?

125. Who finished the clubs highest League scorer with 10 goals?

126. Can you name the Hammers goalkeeper who played in all 38 League games during this season?

127. Who scored West Ham's goal after 33 minutes against Chelsea at Stamford Bridge in a 1-1 League draw?

128. For which club did Matthew Etherington sign when he left Upton Park during January 2009?

129. Which team did The Hammers beat 2-1 at home on the day of the Premier League season?

130. Which Italian forward scored a brace for The Hammers in a 3-1 home win against Newcastle United during September 2008?

PLAYERS' NATIONALITIES

Match the player with his Country of origin

131.	James Collins	Australia
132.	Paolo Di Canio	Czech Republic
133.	Julien Faubert	England
134.	Tomas Repka	Croatia
135.	Javier Mascherano	Italy
136.	Trevor Brooking	France
137.	Slaven Bilic	England
138.	Yossi Benayoun	Wales
139.	Scott Parker	Israel
140.	Stan Lazaridis	Argentina

PLAYERS' TRANSFERS - WHERE DID THEY COME FROM?

Match the player with the team where he signed from to join West Ham

141.	Nolberto Solano	Corinthians
142.	Paolo Di Canio	Liverpool
143.	Carlos Tevez	Newcastle United
144.	Roy Carroll	Arsenal
145.	Christian Dailly	Norwich City
146.	Matthew Etherington	Liverpool
147.	John Hartson	Manchester United
148.	Dean Ashton	Blackburn Rovers
149.	Mike Marsh	Sheffield Wednesday
150.	Neil Ruddock	Tottenham Hotspur

MANAGER: BILLY BONDS

151. Who was Billy appointed manager of in June 1988?

152. In what year was Billy appointed Hammers' boss?

153. To what position in West Ham's first Premier League season did Billy guide them?

154. Billy guided West Ham to promotion to Division One in 1991. To which side did West Ham finish runner-up?

155. Who was West Ham manager before Billy was appointed?

156. What "Tim" and "Iain" did Billy sign during the 1990-1991 season from Luton Town?

157. In 1992, from which club did Billy sign Matt Holmes?

158. Who did West Ham play against in Billy's last game in charge of West Ham?

159. What was Billy's last season in charge at West Ham?

160. Who took over as West Ham manager when Billy resigned?

MARLON HAREWOOD

161. From What club did West Ham sign Marlon?

162. Marlon made his Hammers debut in 2003, against who?

163. Following on from question 162, what was the score in that match?

164. To what club did Marlon go on loan during the season 1998-1999?

165. In what year was Marlon born - 1975, 1977 or 1979?

166. In March 2004 Marlon scored two goals in a 4-2 win, against who?

167. Against which Midlands club did Marlon score in a 1-1 draw in December 2003?

168. In March 2004 against which London club did Marlon score a penalty?

169. Against which Essex side did Marlon score two goals in a 2-0 League Cup win in August 2004?

170. Against which Midlands side did Marlon score a Premier League hat-trick in September 2005 in a 4-0 win?

RIO FERDINAND

171. Where was Rio born - London, Leeds or Manchester?

172. In what position does Rio play?

173. Rio made his West Ham debut in 1996, against who?

174. In what year did Rio win his first England cap?

175. When Rio left West Ham he joined Leeds United for a British record fee - how much?

176. In July 2002 Rio joined Manchester United and become the most expensive British footballer in history. How much did he cost Manchester United?

177. Can you name the season in which Rio won "Hammer of the Year"?

178. During the 1996-1997 season Rio scored two goals for the Hammers. Who were they against?

179. In how many of West Ham's 38 Premier League games during the 1997-1998 season did Rio play - 30, 33 or 35?

180. In which European competition did Rio play for West Ham during July and August 1999?

PLAY-OFF FINAL
WINNERS 2005

181.   Who did West Ham play in the play-off final?

182.   Who scored for West Ham?

183.   Where was the final held?

184.   Can you name the three substitutes that West Ham used in the match?

185.   Name the two West Ham goalkeepers who played in the match.

186.   Can you name the two unused subs?

187.   Can you name the two centre forwards for West Ham who started the match?

188.   Can you name the referee who took control of the match?

189.   Name the manager of the opponents.

190.   Which manager led the Hammers to this success and entering the Premier League?

WEST HAM UNITED - 1980s

191. Can you name the player who scored a hat-trick in a 3-0 win against Queens Park Rangers in April 1981?

192. How old was Billy Bonds when he played his final game for West Ham in April 1988?

193. Who was the top goalscorer during the 1988-1989 season, scoring 7 League, 2 FA Cup and 2 League goals?

194. Which player scored four penalties during the 1987-1988 season?

195. Can you name the player who scored a hat-trick in a 3-1 win against Coventry City in January 1987?

196. West Ham beat Newcastle United 8-1 in April 1986. Which player scored a hat-trick?

197. During the 1981-1982 season, who did West Ham sign from New York Cosmos?

198. During the 1980-1981 season West Ham won the Division 2 Championship. How many games did they win?

199. In what position in the League did West Ham finish during the 1985-1986 season?

200. What was West Ham's biggest win during the 1981-1982 season?

JOE COLE

201. In what year was Joe born - 1981, 1982 or 1983?

202. Which manager gave Joe his West Ham debut?

203. Who did Joe make his Hammers debut against in January 1999?

204. Against which Midlands club did Joe score his first West Ham goal in the League Cup in November 1999?

205. During the 2000-2001 season Joe scored five Premier League goals. Can you name three of the five clubs he scored against?

206. In what season did Joe win "Hammer of the Year"?

207. In January 2002 West Ham beat Macclesfield Town in the FA Cup 3rd round. Joe scored one of the goals, but who scored the other two?

208. In what position in the Premier League did West Ham finish in Joe's first season, 1998-1999?

209. In what year did Joe leave Upton Park?

210. Which club did Joe join when he left West Ham?

MARTIN PETERS

211. In which year was Martin born - 1942, 1943 or 1944?

212. In which position did Martin play?

213. Which manager described Martin as being "ten years ahead of his time"?

214. In which year did Martin make his England debut?

215. England beat West Germany 4-2 in the 1966 World Cup Final. How many goals did Martin score - 1, 2 or 3?

216. In March 1970 West Ham sold Martin to Tottenham Hotspur for a record-breaking fee - how much was it?

217. When Martin moved to Tottenham Hotspur, which player signed for West Ham as part of the deal?

218. Martin made his West Ham debut in 1962 - against who?

219. Apart from the World Cup Final, in what other cup final did Martin play during 1966?

220. For what East Anglian side did Martin play at the end of his career?

LIAM BRADY

221. In what year was Liam born - 1955, 1956 or 1957?

222. In which year did Liam sign for West Ham?

223. Where did West Ham sign Liam from?

224. Liam made his Hammers debut in a 2-0 home defeat, against who?

225. For which North London side did Liam play during the 1970s?

226. How many goals did Liam score during his first season at West Ham?

227. Liam played in three consecutive FA Cup finals - 1978 against Ipswich, 1980 against West Ham, but who did he play against in 1979?

228. In Liam's second season at West Ham he scored two League goals - which two teams were they against?

229. Which country did Liam represent at full international level?

230. How many international caps did Liam win for his country?

PLAYERS PLAYING FOR THEIR COUNTRY

Match the player with the number of caps he won for England

231.	Trevor Brooking (England)	1 Cap
232.	Phil Parkes (England)	67 Caps
233.	Martin Peters (England)	49 Caps
234.	Ken Brown (England)	108 Caps
235.	Tony Cottee (England)	8 Caps
236.	Alan Devonshire (England)	47 Caps
237.	Geoff Hurst (England)	2 Caps
238.	Frank Lampard, SR (England)	17 Caps
239.	Alvin Martin (England)	7 Caps
240.	Bobby Moore (England)	1 Cap

LEAGUE GOALSCORERS
FOR THE HAMMERS

Match the player with the number of League goals scored for West Ham

241.	Steve Whitton	49 goals
242.	David Kelly	15 goals
243.	Ted Fenton	17 goals
244.	James Ruffell	11 goals
245.	Bobby Gould	6 goals
246.	Frank McAvennie	27 goals
247.	Pat Holland	159 goals
248.	Clive Allen	7 goals
249.	Graham Paddon	23 goals
250.	Stuart Slater	11 goals

FRANK McAVENNIE

251. Where was Frank born - Glasgow, London or Manchester?

252. Who did Frank make his Hammers debut against?

253. Frank scored twice on his home debut. Who were the opponents?

254. Where did West Ham sign Frank from in 1985?

255. Frank played in 41 of West Ham's 42 League games during the 1985-1986 season. How many League goals did he score this season?

256. Which Scottish club signed Frank from West Ham during the 1987-1988 season?

257. When John Lyall re-signed Frank in 1989, how much did the Hammers pay?

258. Frank played his final game for West Ham in May 1992, scoring a hat-trick in a 3-0 win, against who?

259. How many League goals did Frank score in his last season at Upton Park?

260. In 1985 Frank made his full Scotland debut, against who?

MANAGER: HARRY REDKNAPP

261. In which year did Harry win the Division Three championship with Bournemouth as manager?

262. What 'Cup' did Harry win as West Ham manager in 1999?

263. In which year did Harry take over as Southampton manager?

264. When Harry took over as manager of Portsmouth in 2002, who did he replace as boss?

265. In which year did Harry join West Ham as assistant manager to Billy Bonds?

266. In which year did Billy Bonds leave as West Ham manager for Harry to take over as boss?

267. Who was Harry's assistant manager at Portsmouth?

268. In what season did Harry lead West Ham to 5th in the Premier League, qualifying for the UEFA Cup?

269. How many of the 42 Premier League games during the 1994-1995 season did Harry win as boss of West Ham?

270. In what season did Harry lead West Ham to a 1-1 draw against Manchester United, denying them a third successive Premier League title?

CLYDE BEST

271. What nationality is Clyde?

272. Which national team did Clyde manage during the 1990s?

273. In 1969 Clyde made his Hammers debut, against who?

274. How many goals did Clyde score in his first season for West Ham?

275. How many League goals did Clyde score for West Ham overall - 43, 45 or 47?

276. Clyde was the second black player to make the Hammers' first team - who was the first?

277. In what season was Clyde West Ham's top goalscorer with 17 League, 2 FA Cup and 4 League Cup goals?

278. For which Dutch club did Clyde play during the 1977-1978 season?

279. Which North American soccer league did Clyde sign for when he left Upton Park?

280. Against which club did Clyde score two goals in the 1971-1972 League Cup quarter-final?

LEAGUE GOALSCORERS
FOR THE HAMMERS

Match the player with the number of League goals scored

281.	Billy Bonds	10 goals
282.	Trevor Brooking	1 goal
283.	Geoff Hurst	3 goals
284.	Malcolm Allison	54 goals
285.	Len Goulden	180 goals
286.	Alvin Martin	94 goals
287.	Joe Cockroft	88 goals
288.	Bryan 'Pop' Robson	62 goals
289.	Ray Stewart	48 goals
290.	Albert Cadwell	27 goals

TONY GALE

291. Who was the referee that sent Tony off in the 1991 FA Cup semi-final against Nottingham Forest?

292. Where was Tony born - London, Manchester or Liverpool?

293. How many League appearances did Tony make for West Ham overall - 200, 300 or 400?

294. How many League goals did Tony score for West Ham overall - 2, 3 or 5?

295. Where did West Ham sign Tony from?

296. What season was Tony's first for the Hammers?

297. What was Tony's nickname at Upton Park?

298. Which manager appointed Tony captain of Fulham at the age of 18?

299. Which manager signed Tony and gave him his Hammers debut?

300. When Tony had his testimonial game in 1994, who was the game against?

PLAYERS' LEAGUE APPEARANCES FOR WEST HAM

Match the player with the number of League appearances made for West Ham

301. Geoff Hurst

302. John Sissons

303. Richard Walker

304. Stan Earle

305. Pat Holland

306. Julian Dicks

307. Tony Gale

308. Paul Goddard

309. George Parris

310. Bobby Moore

211 (28)

293 (7)

159 (11)

410 (1)

543 (1)

258

292

210 (3)

227 (18)

262

STUART PEARCE

311. Can you name three of Stuart's former clubs?

312. How many goals did Stuart score for England?

313. In which year was Stuart awarded the MBE for services to football?

314. Stuart made his West Ham debut in August 1999, against who?

315. Following on from question 314, what was the score in the game?

316. How many goals did Stuart score in his first season for West Ham?

317. For which club did Stuart play before joining West Ham?

318. During 2000-2001 Stuart scored two Premier League goals for the Hammers, against who?

319. Stuart scored for the Hammers in March 2001 in the FA Cup, against who?

320. When Stuart left West Ham who did he join?

PLAYERS' LEAGUE APPEARANCES FOR WEST HAM

Match the player with the number of League appearances made for West Ham

321. Fred Blackburn   344

322. Tommy Yews   340

323. John Bond   505

324. Jimmy Ruffell   302

325. Phil Parkes   251

326. George Kay   346

327. Martin Peters   217

328. Peter Brabrook   381

329. Tommy Taylor   237

330. Joe Cockroft   167

PAUL INCE

331. Where was Paul born - London, Manchester or Birmingham?

332. Paul was the first black player to have done what?

333. Paul made his debut for West Ham in a 4-0 defeat, against who?

334. When Paul left West Ham, who did he join?

335. Against which team did Paul make his England debut?

336. Which cup did Manchester United win in Paul's first season, giving him his first of many trophies with United?

337. What was Paul's nickname at Old Trafford?

338. Which Italian side did Paul sign for when he left Manchester United?

339. How many England caps did Paul win - 51, 52 or 53?

340. When Paul left Liverpool, which Premier League side did he sign for?

PAOLO DI CANIO

341. What nationality is Paolo?

342. In which year was Paolo born - 1966, 1967 or 1968?

343. For which Scottish team did Paolo play?

344. When Paolo left Scotland he went to play for which Premier League team?

345. In 1998 Paolo pushed a referee to the ground after being sent off - who was the referee?

346. In which year did Paolo sign for the Hammers - 1997, 1998 or 1999?

347. In 2000 Paolo scored a fantastic volley for the Hammers, which is considered one of the best goals in Premier League history - which team was this against?

348. In 2001 which award did Paolo win?

349. Which London club signed Paolo in 2003 when he left West Ham?

350. In 2004 Paolo left England to return home to Italy to play for which side?

STEVE POTTS

351.   What is Steve's nickname?

352.   In which year did Steve join West Ham as an apprentice?

353.   How many goals did Steve score in his West Ham career?

354.   In which country was Steve born?

355.   Against which club did Steve play against on his West Ham debut in 1985?

356.   Can you name the two seasons in which Steve won "Hammer of the Year"?

357.   Who did Steve score against in a 7-1 win in October 1990?

358.   Steve played in all 46 League matches during the 1992-1993 season. Who were the only other two players to do so?

359.   Which Hammers manager gave Steve his debut?

360.   Steve was the only West Ham player to have done what during the 1994-1995 season?

FA CUP WINNERS - 1975

361. Who did West Ham beat in the Cup Final?

362. What was the score?

363. Who scored West Ham's goals?

364. From where did West Ham sign their Cup Final goalscorer?

365. Going into this Cup Final West Ham had just finished their 42 League matches. How many did they win - 12, 13 or 14?

366. Who played in goal for the Hammers?

367. Going into this FA Cup Final, how many FA Cups had West Ham won?

368. Who was the referee?

369. Which manager led West Ham to this success?

370. Which two former England captains were playing for the opponents?

PAUL GODDARD

371. In what year was Paul born - 1955, 1957 or 1959?

372. Which manager signed Paul for West Ham?

373. When Paul signed for West Ham it was for a club record fee of £800,000. Where did he sign from?

374. Paul made his debut for West Ham in 1980 in the Charity Shield, against who?

375. How many League appearances did Paul make for West Ham - 100, 140 or 170?

376. How many League goals did Paul score for the Hammers overall - 14, 54 or 104?

377. Paul's final appearance for West Ham was in 1986, against who?

378. When Paul left West Ham, who did he join?

379. For which East Anglian side has Paul played in his career?

380. Paul won one cap for England in 1982, against who?

GEOFF HURST

381. Geoff is the only player to have done what in a World Cup final?

382. How many goals did Geoff score for England?

383. In which year did Geoff retire from playing?

384. For which county cricket side did Geoff play?

385. In which year was Geoff knighted?

386. When Geoff left West Ham, who did he sign for?

387. In what year did Geoff leave West Ham?

388. How many League goals did Geoff score for West Ham overall - 80, 180 or 280?

389. How many League appearances did Geoff make for West Ham?

390. Who did Geoff score his first West Ham goal against in a 4-2 home win?

MANAGER: ALAN PARDEW

391. In what year was Alan appointed manager at West Ham?

392. When Alan was appointed manager at Reading, who did he take over from?

393. Which caretaker manager did Alan take over from at Upton Park when he arrived?

394. In what year was Alan born - 1957, 1959 or 1961?

395. When Alan left Crystal Palace during his playing career, who did he join?

396. What player was Alan's first signing for West Ham?

397. Against which club did West Ham play in Alan's first Premier League game in charge of West Ham?

398. Alan scored the winner for Crystal Palace in the 1990 FA Cup semi-final, against who?

399. Which club did West Ham play in the 2004 play-off final which Alan guided West Ham to?

400. Alan left Upton Park in December 2006, which London based Premier League team did he go on to manage in the same month as he left West Ham?

DAVID CROSS

401.   In what year was David born - 1940, 1950 or 1960?

402.   Where did West Ham sign David from?

403.   How much did West Ham pay for David?

404.   Against which club did David play on his Hammers debut?

405.   What was David's nickname?

406.   For which East Anglian side has David played in his career?

407.   How many goals did David score in his first full season at Upton Park?

408.   David scored in his last match for West Ham in 1982. Who was this against?

409.   David twice scored four goals in a game. Can you name both clubs he scored against for the Hammers?

410.   How many League goals did David score in his West Ham career - 77, 79 or 81?

ALAN CURBISHLEY

411. In which year did Alan begin his career as an apprentice with West Ham?

412. For which two Midlands clubs did Alan play during his playing career?

413. Which manager did Alan replace at Upton Park in 2006?

414. Alan was appointed joint Charlton manager in 1991, with who?

415. In what year did Alan guide Charlton to the Division One title to get them promoted to the Premier League?

416. Against which club did Alan make his Hammers debut?

417. When Alan left West Ham as a player, who did he join?

418. Alan was appointed West Ham manager in December 2006, against which team did Alan record his first win as manager of the Hammers in his first game in charge?

419. How many League appearances did Alan make for West Ham - 85, 95 or 105?

420. How many goals did Alan score for the Hammers in his West Ham career - 10, 11 or 12?

CHRISTIAN DAILLY

421. What nationality is Christian?

422. Can you name the club from which Christian was signed for the Hammers?

423. Where was Christian born - Dundee, Leeds or Cardiff?

424. How many under-21 caps did Christian win for his country - 31, 32 or 34?

425. When Christian signed for Derby County, which club did he sign from?

426. Which national manager gave Christian his first senior cap for his country?

427. Christian scored on his second full international match - against who?

428. What season was Christian's first at Upton Park?

429. What manager signed Christian for West Ham?

430. Christian was the only West Ham player to have done what during the 2001-2002 season?

DAVID JAMES

431. In what year was David born - 1968, 1969 or 1970?

432. Where did Liverpool sign David from?

433. Which manager signed David for Liverpool?

434. Which club did David sign for when he left Liverpool in 1999?

435. In what year did David sign for the Hammers?

436. In 2004 David left West Ham and signed for who?

437. Against Which country did David make his England debut?

438. David played under Glenn Roeder in 1992, for which club?

439. How many League appearances did David make in his first season at Upton Park - 20, 23 or 26?

440. Which manager signed David for the Hammers?

BILLY BONDS

441. Where was Billy born - London, Manchester or Liverpool?

442. From which club did Billy Bonds join West Ham in 1967?

443. Billy Bonds was appointed captain of the Hammers after the departure of who?

444. Billy Bonds is the only West Ham captain to have done what on two occasions?

445. What was Billy's nickname at West Ham?

446. What is the total number of goals Billy scored for West Ham - 50, 53 or 59?

447. In the 1973-1974 season Billy scored 13 goals including a hat-trick, against who?

448. In which year did Billy receive the MBE from the queen?

449. How many appearances did Billy make for West Ham (in all competitions) - 693, 793 or 893?

450. Billy made his final appearance for West Ham in 1988, against who?

WHAT WAS THE SCORE?

Match the game West Ham played with the final score

451. **Charlton Athletic**
      Premier League, December 2000   **5-2 win**

452. **Leeds United**
      League Cup, November 1966   **3-1 win**

453. **Bristol City**
      League Cup, October 1984   **7-2 win**

454. **Fulham**
      Division 1, February 1968   **6-1 win**

455. **Tottenham Hotspur**
      Premier League, April 1994   **4-4 draw**

456. **Norwich City**
      Division 1, April 1991   **6-1 win**

457. **Coventry City**
      Division 1, November 1981   **5-0 win**

458. **Aldershot**
      FA Cup, January 1991   **4-0 win**

459. **Ararat Erevan**
      European Cup Winners' Cup, November 1975   **7-0 win**

460. **Charlton Athletic**
      Premier League, November 2001   **4-1 win**

HAT-TRICK HEROES

Match the game with the player that scored a hat-trick

461. **Stoke City, November 1957,**
     5-0 win, Division 2   Billy Jennings

462. **West Bromwich Albion, August 1968,**
     4-0 win, Division 1   Paul Goddard

463. **Leicester City, December 1967,**
     4-2 win, Division 1   Francois Van der Elst

464. **Coventry City, September 1983,**
     5-2 win, Division 1   Johnny Dick

465. **Sheffield United, March 1990,**
     5-0 win, Division 2   Paul Kitson

466. **West Bromwich Albion, March 1959,**
     3-1 win, Division 1   Dave Swindlehurst

467. **Sheffield Wednesday, May 1997,**
     5-1 win, Premier League   Jimmy Quinn

468. **Stoke City, December 1975,**
     3-1 win, Division 1   Vic Keeble

469. **Notts County, December 1982,**
     3-3 draw, League Cup   Brian Dear

470. **Port Vale, January 1985,**
     4-1 win, FA Cup   Martin Peters

47

MATTHEW ETHERINGTON

471.   In what year was Matthew born - 1976, 1981 or 1986?

472.   Which club did Matthew sign from to join the Hammers?

473.   Matthew made his West Ham debut against Leicester City in a 0-0 draw, in what year?

474.   In the season 2001-2002, for which club did Matthew play 13 games, scoring one goal, on loan?

475.   In what season was Matthew voted "Hammer of the Year"?

476.   West Ham beat Blackburn Rovers 3-1 on the opening day of the 2005-2006 season, Matthew scored one of the goals, but who scored the other two?

477.   Against which London team did Matthew score a hat-trick in March 2004 in a 5-0 win?

478.   On New Year's Day 2005, Matthew scored a goal in a 2-0 win, against who?

479.   Which squad number did Matthew wear during the 2005-2006 season?

480.   Which manager was in charge of West Ham when Matthew joined the club?

CRAIG FORREST

481. For which country did Craig play in goal?

482. Which club did Craig sign from to join West Ham?

483. In which year did Craig sign for West Ham?

484. How many caps did Craig win for his country?

485. Which Cup did Craig win with his country in 2000?

486. In what position in the League did West Ham finish in Craig's first season at Upton Park?

487. Which was the only Cup competition Craig played in during 1999?

488. Which Hammers manager signed Craig for West Ham?

489. During the 1999-2000 season Craig started nine Premier League matches and made two sub appearances. Which four other goalkeepers played for West Ham in that season?

490. During the 1998-1999 season Craig started one League game for West Ham. What West Ham goalkeeper started the other 37 Premier League matches?

CLIVE ALLEN

491. In what year was Clive born - 1957, 1959 or 1961?

492. In what position did Clive play for West Ham?

493. In 1992, Clive scored on his Hammers debut in a 2-1 defeat. Who was this against?

494. Where did West Ham sign Clive from?

495. For which London club did Clive play between 1984-1988?

496. Which London-based club did Clive sign for when he left West Ham in 1994?

497. Clive made a total of 44 appearances for West Ham scoring how many goals?

498. Clive made his England debut in 1984, against who?

499. In January 1993 Clive scored his only Cup goal for West Ham. Who was it against?

500. Clive made his last appearance for West Ham in a goalless FA Cup quarter-final tie at Upton Park, against who?

LEAGUE CUP FINALISTS - 1966

501. Who did West Ham play in the Cup final?

502. Which team did West Ham beat 10-3 on aggregate in the semi-finals?

503. Can you name the two players that played in all ten League Cup games, including the final?

504. Which player scored in every round of the competition except the final?

505. Can you remember the score in the final, first leg?

506. Can you remember the score in the final, second leg?

507. Which manager guided West Ham to the final?

508. Who captained West Ham during this Cup run, scoring two goals in the competition?

509. Who scored West Ham's goals over the two Cup final legs?

510. Which player scored eleven League Cup goals during the Cup run?

JOHNNY BYRNE

511. *In what year was Johnny born - 1937, 1938 or 1939?*

512. *In 1962 Johnny signed for the Hammers, from which team?*

513. *What was Johnny's nickname at West Ham?*

514. *In what season did Johnny win "Hammer of the Year"?*

515. *Against which club did Johnny score his first West Ham goal in 1962 in a 4-1 win?*

516. *In February 1964 West Ham beat which club 4-3 where Johnny scored a hat-trick?*

517. *Who did Johnny play against in his last appearance for West Ham in 1967?*

518. *In what season did Johnny finish top goalscorer for the Hammers with 25 League, 1 FA Cup, 3 European Cup Winners Cup and 1 Charity Shield goals?*

519. *Against which London club did Johnny score a hat-trick in a 3-2 win in September 1964?*

520. *When Johnny left West Ham, who did he join?*

CARLTON COLE

521. In which year was Carlton born in Surrey – 1981,1982
      or 1983?

522. From which London team did Carlton sign when he
      joined The Hammers?

523. Which squad number did Carlton wear for The
      Hammers during the 2009/2010 season?

524. Which Hammers manager signed Carlton for West Ham
      United?

525. Against which team did Carlton score West Ham's first
      goal in the 2-2 home League draw during October
      2009?

526. True or false: Carlton scored on his Hammers debut in
      a 3-1 home League win?

527. Against which team did Carlton score West Ham's
      winning goal in a 2-1 home League win during April
      2008?

528. Following on from the previous question, who scored
      West Ham's first goal in the game?

529. Which England manager handed Carlton his full
      international debut during 2009?

530. For which club did Carlton play during the 2004/2005
      season, whilst on loan?

ALAN DICKENS

531. Where was Alan born - London, Leicester or Liverpool?

532. In what year did Alan sign as an apprentice for West Ham?

533. What was Alan's nickname at Upton Park?

534. Alan made a goalscoring debut in 1982 for West Ham, against who?

535. How many League appearances did Alan make for West Ham in his career - 190, 192 or 194?

536. How many League goals did Alan score for West Ham in his career - 13, 23 or 33?

537. When Alan left West Ham, who did he join?

538. How many England under-21 caps did Alan win?

539. Alan was part of West Ham's FA Youth Cup winning side in 1981. Who did they beat?

540. For which Essex-based team did Alan play towards the end of his career?

TOMAS REPKA

541. Which Italian side did Tomas sign from to join West Ham?

542. How many times was Tomas sent off during his first three matches for West Ham?

543. Which Hammers manager signed Tomas?

544. Where did Tomas start his career?

545. What was Tomas's first season at West Ham?

546. How much did West Ham pay for Tomas?

547. In how many of West Ham's 38 Premier League games did Tomas play during his first season at Upton Park?

548. For which international team has Tomas played full international matches?

549. Against which country did Tomas make his international debut against?

550. During the 2005-2006 season, what squad number did Tomas wear for West Ham?

PHIL PARKES

551. Which club did West Ham sign Phil from?

552. Which West Ham manager signed Phil?

553. Phil was bought for a world-record fee for a
      goalkeeper - how much money did the Hammers
      spend?

554. How many League appearances did Phil make for the
      Hammers?

555. What was Phil's nickname at West Ham?

556. Who did Phil make his Hammers debut against in
      1979 in a 3-0 home win?

557. In what season did Phil get voted "Hammer of the
      Year"?

558. Which club did Phil join as a goalkeeping coach to be
      reunited with boss John Lyall?

559. During the 1978-1979 season, which two other
      goalkeepers played for West Ham?

560. Phil made his last appearance for West Ham in a 6-0
      defeat. Who were the opponents?

ALVIN MARTIN

561. Where was Alvin born - London, Leeds or Liverpool?

562. Alvin was given two testimonials by West Ham and only one other ex-Hammers player has had two. Who is he?

563. What was Alvin's nickname?

564. How many England caps did Alvin win?

565. Which manager gave Alvin his England debut?

566. In which year did Alvin join West Ham as an apprentice?

567. Against which team did Alvin make his Hammers debut in a 4-1 defeat?

568. In April 1986 West Ham beat Newcastle United 8-1. Alvin scored a hat-trick and scored against three different goalkeepers in the match - can you name them?

569. In the 1993-1994 season Alvin scored two goals for West Ham in their first Premier League season. Who were the goals against?

570. When Alvin left West Ham during the summer of 1996, who did he join?

FRANK LAMPARD (SNR)

571. Where was Frank born - London, Glasgow or Cardiff?

572. In which year did Frank make his West Ham debut?

573. Frank made his full England debut in 1972, against who?

574. How many FA Cup winners medals did Frank win with West Ham?

575. Which club did Frank join when he left the Hammers?

576. From 1994 to 2001 Frank was assistant manager to who at Upton Park?

577. Who did Frank make his West Ham debut against?

578. Frank made his final West Ham appearance in 1985, against who?

579. How many League appearances did Frank make in his West Ham career - 515, 551 or 555?

580. In 1980 Frank scored in the FA Cup semi-final at Elland Road and in celebration he danced around the corner flag. Who was this against?

WEST HAM UNITED - POT LUCK

581. West Ham were first formed as 'Thames Iron Works Football Club'. Which year was this - 1894, 1895 or 1896?

582. In which year did West Ham start playing at Upton Park - 1903, 1904 or 1905?

583. In which year was the club formed as 'West Ham United Football Club' - 1898, 1899 or 1900?

584. Which season was West Ham's first in the Premier League - 1992-1993, 1993-1994 or 1994-1995?

585. What are West Ham's colours?

586. In which part of London are West Ham situated?

587. West Ham's record attendance was over 42,000 in 1970 - against who?

588. What was West Ham's highest ever position in the old First Division, which was achieved in 1985-1986?

589. West Ham's record League victory in the 1968-1969 season was 8-0, against who?

590. West Ham's record victory in European competition was against Castilla in 1980. What was the score?

TIM BREAKER

591. In what year was Tim born - 1963, 1964 or 1965?

592. How many England under-21 caps did he win?

593. Where did Tim sign from to join West Ham?

594. Which manager signed Tim to become the manager's first signing in 1990?

595. Who did Tim make his West Ham debut against?

596. Tim scored one goal during his first season at Upton Park. Who did he score against?

597. During the 1994-1995 season, how many of the 42 League games did he play - 31, 33 or 35?

598. Tim scored three goals in West Ham's first Premier League season, against which clubs?

599. When Tim left West Ham, which club did he join?

600. How many goals did Tim score in his West Ham career?

MANAGER: LOU MACARI

601. Where was Lou born - Edinburgh, Glasgow or London?

602. Lou was an attacking midfield player for Manchester United. Where did he sign from?

603. When he made his debut for Manchester United, who was it against?

604. In 1977 Lou scored the winner in the FA Cup final for Manchester United, against who?

605. In which year did Lou take over as West Ham manager?

606. How many managers had West Ham had before Lou?

607. Which Scottish team did Lou manage during the 1993-1994 season?

608. How many Scottish caps did Lou win for Scotland during his playing career - 18, 21 or 24?

609. Which team did Lou manage between 1991-1993 and then again between 1994-1997?

610. Who took over as West Ham manager when Lou left Upton Park?

FREDERIC KANOUTE

611.   From which club did West Ham sign Frederic?

612.   During the 1999-2000 season Frederic made eight
       Premier League appearances for the Hammers.
       How many goals did he score - 2, 4 or 6?

613.   Following on from question 612, which teams did
       Frederic score against?

614.   Which London side did West Ham beat on Boxing
       Day 2000, winning 5-0, with Frederic scoring twice?

615.   Frederic was West Ham's highest scorer during the
       2000-2001 season with how many goals (in all
       comps)?

616.   For which team did Frederic play in the African Cup of
       Nations during 2004?

617.   Which London side did Frederic score against in the FA
       Cup in January 2002 in a 1-1 draw?

618.   Against which midlands club did Frederic score two
       goals in January 2001 in the FA Cup in a 3-2 win?

619.   In what year did West Ham sell Frederic to London
       rivals Tottenham?

620.   In August 2005 Spurs sold Frederic to which club?

WEST HAM UNITED - POT LUCK

621. Who was the only player to play in every Premier League match during the 2000-2001 season?

622. When Andy Impey left West Ham, who did he join?

623. During the 1970-1971 season Bobby Moore and Jimmy Greaves were suspended by the Hammers. Why?

624. During the 1959-1960 season West Ham signed Dave Dunmore. Where from?

625. How many of the 42 Premier League matches did West Ham win during their first season in the top flight (1993-1994) - 11, 12 or 13?

626. Can you name the two clubs that West Ham played in the UEFA Cup during the 1999-2000 season?

627. From what team did West Ham sign Jimmy Greaves?

628. Who signed for West Ham from Espanol in 1996?

629. Who managed West Ham during the early 1900s?

630. Where did West Ham sign Scott Minto from?

MERVYN DAY

631. In what year was Mervyn born - 1950, 1955 or 1960?

632. In what year did Mervyn make his Hammers debut?

633. Who did Mervyn make his West Ham debut against?

634. For which goalkeeper did Mervyn come on as substitute to make his Hammers debut?

635. Mervyn's final appearance for the Hammers was in a 3-3 draw, against who?

636. When Mervyn left West Ham, who did he join in 1979?

637. What award did Mervyn win in 1975?

638. Mervyn won an FA Cup medal in 1975. Who did West Ham beat in the final 2-0?

639. For which Midlands club did Mervyn play during his career?

640. At what London-based Premier League club was Mervyn appointed assistant manager to Alan Curbishley?

2004-2005 RESULTS
IN THE CHAMPIONSHIP

Match the Championship game with the final score

641.	*v. Plymouth Argyle (H)*	**Drew 0-0**
642.	*v. Nottingham Forest (H)*	**Won 2-1**
643.	*v. Cardiff City (A)*	**Lost 2-1**
644.	*v. Ipswich Town (H)*	**Won 3-2**
645.	*v. Brighton & Hove Albion (A)*	**Won 5-0**
646.	*v. Sunderland (A)*	**Drew 1-1**
647.	*v. Leicester City (A)*	**Won 3-2**
648.	*v. Watford (H)*	**Lost 4-1**
649.	*v. Watford (A)*	**Drew 2-2**
650.	*v. Leeds United (A)*	**Won 2-0**

MARK WARD

651. Where was Mark born - London, Liverpool or Leeds?

652. Where did Mark sign from to join West Ham?

653. How much did the Hammers pay for Mark?

654. Who did Mark make his Hammers debut against in August 1985?

655. How many goals did he score in his first season at Upton Park in Division 1?

656. Mark moved to Manchester City in 1989. Which two players joined West Ham from Manchester City as part of the deal?

657. Which team did he sign for when he left Manchester City?

658, Under what manager did he play for Manchester City and Everton?

659. Which Midlands side did Mark sign for in March 1994?

660. In what position did Mark play?

JOE KIRKUP

661.   In what year was Joe born - 1935, 1937 or 1939?

662.   Joe made his West Ham debut in 1958 in a 3-1 defeat, against who?

663.   Against which club did Joe score his first goal for West Ham?

664.   In Joe's first season at Upton Park (1958-1959), how many League appearances did he make?

665.   How many League goals did Joe score for West Ham in his Hammers career?

666.   Against which East Anglian club did Joe score against in a 2-2 draw in February 1962?

667.   How many appearances did Joe make for West Ham in his Hammers career (in all comps) - 108, 187 or 238?

668.   For how much did West Ham sell Joe in 1966?

669.   In 1975 to which country did Joe move to join Durban City as player/manager?

670.   Who did Joe join when he left West Ham in 1966?

PLAYERS' TRANSFERS:
WHERE DID THEY GO?

Match the player with the club he joined on leaving West Ham

671.	Carl Fletcher	Manchester City
672.	Clyde Best	Fulham
673.	Lee Chapman	Tampa Bay Rowdies
674.	Stewart Robson	Leyton Orient
675.	Slaven Bilic	Crystal Palace
676.	David Cross	Ipswich Town
677.	Bobby Moore	Birmingham City
678.	George Parris	Everton
679.	Kevin Lock	Coventry City
680.	Mervyn Day	Fulham

JERMAIN DEFOE

681. *In what year was Jermain born - 1978, 1980 or 1982?*

682. *For which club did Jermain play, on loan, during the 2000-2001 season?*

683. *Jermain scored on his West Ham debut - against who?*

684. *How many League goals did Jermain score during the 2001-2002 season - 8, 9 or 10?*

685. *Against which side did Jermain score a hat-trick in September 2003 in League Cup competition?*

686. *What squad number did Jermain wear during the 2002-2003 season?*

687. *Which team did England play when Jermain made his international debut?*

688. *Who did Jermain sign for when he left Upton Park?*

689. *Which player signed for West Ham as part of the deal for Jermain?*

690. *Jermain scored his first England goal in September 2004, against who?*

WEST HAM UNITED - 1960s

691. In December 1962 West Ham drew 4-4 with Spurs. Can you name the four goalscorers?

692. Who was West Ham's highest goalscorer with 13 League and 2 League Cup goals during the 1962-1963 season?

693. Which player scored five goals in a 6-1 win over West Bromwich Albion in April 1965?

694. In the 1960-1961 season West Ham had two managers. Can you name them both?

695. In the 1964-1965 season, how many League games did West Ham win - 17, 18 or 19?

696. West Ham played Liverpool in the 1964 Charity Shield. What was the score?

697. Following on from question 696, who scored West Ham's goals?

698. In October 1968 West Ham beat Sunderland 8-0. Which player scored six of the goals?

699. In November 1961 Bobby Moore was sent off against Manchester City. What was the score in the match?

700. Which 17-year-old made his debut for West Ham in a 5-2 win against Preston North End in 1960?

RAY STEWART

701. In what year was Ray born - 1957, 1958 or 1959?

702. In what position did Ray play?

703. How old was Ray when he made his West Ham debut?

704. Ray made his debut in 1979 in a 1-1 draw, against who?

705. Where did West Ham sign Ray from?

706. How many League goals did Ray score for West Ham in his Hammers career - 42, 52 or 62?

707. What was Ray's nickname at Upton Park?

708. Ray won ten caps for Scotland. The first cap was in 1981, against who?

709. How many League goals did Ray score in his first season at Upton Park - 8, 9 or 10?

710. When Ray left West Ham, who did he join?

FA CUP WINNERS - 1964

711. Who did West Ham play against in the FA Cup final?

712. What was the score in the game?

713. Can you name the two London sides that West Ham beat to reach the final, playing them in rounds 3 and 4?

714. Who did the Hammers beat 3-1 in the semi-final?

715. Which players scored the semi-final goals?

716. At what stadium was the semi-final played?

717. Who scored seven FA Cup goals during this Cup run?

718. Who played in goal for West Ham in the final?

719. In what month was the FA Cup final played at Wembley?

720. Can you name the West Ham goalscorers that scored in the final?

NEIL ORR

721. In what year was Neil born - 1955, 1957 or 1959?

722. Where did West Ham sign Neil from?

723. Neil signed for the Hammers in 1982. How much was the fee?

724. Neil made his debut in 1982, against who?

725. In October 1983 who did Neil score against in a 2-1 win in the League Cup?

726. How many of West Ham's 42 League matches did Neil start during the 1985-1986 season?

727. For what Scottish club did Neil play during the 1993-1994 season?

728. How many Scotland under-23 caps did Neil win - 5, 6 or 7?

729. During the 1985-1986 season Neil scored two League goals against which two sides?

730. When Neil left West Ham, who did he join in 1987?

MANAGER: GLENN ROEDER

731. Which two teams had Glenn managed before West Ham?

732. To what position in the League did Glenn guide West Ham in his first season in charge?

733. Who did Glenn take over from as Hammers boss?

734. How many of the 38 Premier League games did Glenn win as manager during the 2001-2002 season?

735. Who did Glenn replace Les Sealey with as goalkeeping coach when he took over as boss?

736. When Glenn took over as Hammers boss, who did he appoint as his assistant manager?

737. What Czech international defender did Glenn sign in his first season in charge?

738. Can you name the strike partnership that scored 26 goals (in all competitions) in Glenn's first season at Upton Park?

739. Can you name two of the four clubs that Glenn played for during his playing career?

740. Shortly after leaving West Ham, which Premier League club did Glenn join as a coach?

IAIN DOWIE

741. Which team did Iain leave as manager to join Crystal Palace?

742. Which team did Iain manage for two games in 1998?

743. Which West Ham manager brought Iain to Upton Park in 1991?

744. Iain made his Hammers debut in 1991, against who?

745. Where did West Ham sign Iain from in 1991?

746. In Iain's first season (1990-1991) at West Ham, how many League goals did he score - 3, 4 or 5?

747. Which manager re-signed Iain in 1995 to bring him back to Upton Park for a second spell?

748. How many goals did Iain score during the 1995-1996 season (in all competitions) - 9, 11 or 13?

749. Can you name the side that Iain scored two goals against in a 4-2 win in March 1996?

750. In October 1996, Iain scored twice in the League Cup 3rd round in a 4-1 win. Who were the opponents?

GEORGE PARRIS

751.   In what year did George sign for West Ham as an apprentice?

752.   George made his debut in 1985 for West Ham, against who?

753.   What was George's nickname at Upton Park?

754.   Who did George score his first West Ham goal against in a 4-0 win?

755.   Against which London club did George score in the FA Cup in 1987?

756.   How many goals did George score for West Ham during the 1990-1991 season (in all comps)?

757.   How many goals did George score in his career at West Ham (in all comps)?

758.   During the 1990-1991 season George was voted "Hammer of the Year" runner-up. Who won the award?

759.   How many League appearances did George make for the Hammers - 230, 233 or 239?

760.   When George left West Ham, which club did he join, costing them £100,000?

MICHAEL CARRICK

761.   Who did Michael score his first goal against for West Ham in a 5-0 win?

762.   In which cup competition did Michael make a sub appearance in 1999?

763.   Who did Michael make his West Ham debut against?

764.   Which Midlands club did Michael score against in a 1-1 draw in December 2000?

765.   In what year was Michael born - 1981, 1982 or 1983?

766.   Michael was given his full England debut in 2001, against who?

767.   Against which two teams did Michael score against the 2001-2002 season for West Ham?

768.   To which Midlands side was Michael loaned in 1999?

769.   In what season was Michael voted "Hammer of the Year" runner-up to Matthew Etherington?

770.   Who did Michael join when he left West Ham?

FA CUP WINNERS - 1980

771.   Who did West Ham play in the FA Cup final?

772.   What was the score in the game?

773.   Which West Ham player scored in this game?

774.   In what minute was the goal scored?

775.   Which manager guided West Ham to victory?

776.   Who played in goal for the Hammers?

777.   Which player become the youngest person to appear in an FA Cup final?

778.   What London club did West Ham knock out in round 4, beating them 3-2?

779.   Who scored three FA Cup goals to help West Ham get to the final?

780.   Which club did West Ham beat 2-1 in the semi-final replay to reach the final?

FRANK LAMPARD (JNR)

781. In what year was Frank born?

782. Which club was Frank loaned out to in October 1995 from West Ham?

783. Who did Frank make his West Ham debut against in 1996?

784. Frank scored his first West Ham goal in the 1996-1997 season, against who?

785. How many England under-21 caps did Frank win - 15, 17 or 19?

786. In November 1997 Frank scored a hat-trick in the League Cup in a 4-1 win, against who?

787. During the 1998-1999 season what was Frank the only West Ham player to have done?

788. In September 1999 Frank scored for the Hammers in the UEFA Cup in a 3-0 win, against who?

789. Frank played six Intertoto matches during July and August 1999. How many goals did he score?

790. Against which country did Frank score a penalty against for England in a 1-0 win in October 2005?

PAT HOLLAND

791. Where was Pat born - Leicester, London or Liverpool?

792. During the season 1970-1971 Pat was sent out on loan to which club, making ten appearances?

793. What was Pat's nickname at Upton Park?

794. During the 1969-1970 season Pat scored one League goal for West Ham in a 1-0 win, against who?

795. What season was Pat's last at West Ham, making 25 appearances?

796. Which club did Pat join in 1988 to coach their youth and reserve teams?

797. Which two "United's" did Pat score against in the League during the 1973-1974 season?

798. How many League goals did Pat score in his West Ham career?

799. Against which club did Pat play in his testimonial?

800. When Pat left Upton Park in 1984, who did he join as player/coach?

WEST HAM UNITED - 1970s

801. Which player scored twice on his debut against Manchester City in March 1970 in a 5-1 win?

802. Bobby Moore won his 100th England cap in 1973. Who did England play?

803. During the 1974-1975 season West Ham's biggest win was against Tranmere Rovers. What was the score?

804. In March 1978 which player scored a hat-trick against Ipswich Town in a 3-0 win?

805. What was West Ham's biggest win during 1971-1972?

806. Which player was the highest goalscorer in 1971-1972 with 17 League, 2 FA Cup and 4 League Cup goals?

807. Can you name two of the four players that never missed a League game during the 1971-1972 season?

808. Can you name the only player that did not miss a game during the 1975-1976 season?

809. In what Division were West Ham during 1978-1979?

810. Which player was the highest goalscorer during the 1970-1971 season with a total of 16 goals?

WEST HAM UNITED - POT LUCK

811. What is the title of the song that is associated with West Ham, which the fans sing at each match?

812. Which London side did West Ham beat 5-0 in December 2000, making it their best win that season?

813. Who was West Ham captain during the 1985-1986 season?

814. Where did West Ham sign Ian Pearce from?

815. Which Scottish striker was on loan to the Hammers during the 1992-1993 season, making eleven appearances and scoring four goals?

816. Which former Tottenham full-back signed for West Ham in 1990, making his debut against Notts County?

817. Where did West Ham sign Paulo Futre from?

818. During West Ham's Division 2 Championship success, there were only two players that played in all 42 League matches. Can you name them?

819. From which club did West Ham sign Davor Suker from?

820. Who did West Ham sell Marc-Vivien Foe to?

WEST HAM IN THE FA CUP

821. Which Welsh club knocked West Ham out of the 1981 FA Cup competition after a second replay?

822. Who did West Ham lose to, 2-0, in the quarter-final during the 1985 FA Cup run?

823. Jermain Defoe scored four goals in the 2002 FA Cup run. Which two clubs did he score his goals against?

824. Where did West Ham play their semi-final match against Nottingham Forest in the 1991 FA Cup?

825. During the 1998 FA Cup, West Ham got as far as the quarter-finals, but Arsenal beat the Hammers 6-5 on penalties. Which West Ham player missed the last one?

826. Which Essex side did West Ham beat 2-0 in the 1996 FA Cup?

827. Which two Midlands clubs did West Ham knock out on their run to the 1980 FA Cup final?

828. Which team beat West Ham 3-2 in 2002 in a 4th round replay in which Jermain Defoe scored both goals?

829. Which two London-based clubs did the Hammers knock out during the 1999 FA Cup run?

830. Only four players played in all eight games during the 1980 FA Cup run. Who were they?

DON HUTCHISON

831. In what year was Don born - 1971, 1973 or 1975?

832. In Don's first spell at West Ham, he made his debut in 1994 scoring in a 3-1 defeat at home, against who?

833. In 1994, West Ham paid £1.5 million for Don. Which club did they sign him from?

834. What was Don's nickname at Upton Park?

835. Which manager brought Don to Upton Park in 1994?

836. During the 1995-1996 season Don scored two Premier League goals for the Hammers against which two London sides?

837. Don left West Ham during the 1995-1996 season. Who did he sign for?

838. Which Hammers manager signed Don in 2001 to join West Ham from Sunderland for his second spell?

839. Don scored one Premier League goal for West Ham during the 2001-2002 season in a 3-0 win, against who?

840. How many Premier League goals did Don score for West Ham during the 1994-1995 season - 5, 7 or 9?

WEST HAM UNITED - 1990s

841. Which player was top goalscorer during the 1990-1991 season with 12 League, 4 FA Cup and 1 League goals?

842. Which two players captained West Ham during the 1991-1992 season?

843. Who was the first West Ham player to score a hat-trick in the Premier League in December 1994?

844. During the 1995-1996 season West Ham scored five League penalties. Which player scored all of them?

845. Which player scored a hat-trick in a 5-1 win over Sheffield Wednesday in May 1997?

846. Which ex-Arsenal legend was top goalscorer with nine League goals during the 1998-1999 season?

847. Can you name the midfielder who played in all 38 Premier League matches during the 1998-1999 season?

848. West Ham finished 5th in the Premier League during the 1998-1999 season. What competition did they qualify for?

849. Which player was top goalscorer during the 1997-1998 season with 15 League, 3 FA Cup and 6 League Cup goals?

850. Who was the only player to play in every League game during the 1990-1991 season?

WEST HAM IN CUP COMPETITIONS

Match the Hammers' competition placing with the year in which it was achieved

851.	FA Cup Finalists	1966
852.	League Cup Finalists	1991
853.	FA Cup Winners	1976
854.	European Cup Winners' Cup Finalists	1965
855.	FA Cup Winners	2006
856.	League Cup Finalists	1964
857.	European Cup Winners' Cup Winners	1923
858.	FA Cup Winners	1981
859.	FA Cup Finalists	1980
860.	FA Cup Semi-Finalists	1975

MANAGER: JOHN LYALL

861. In what year was John appointed manager of West Ham?

862. Which manager did John take over from at West Ham?

863. What position in Division One did West Ham finish in John's first season in charge?

864. What Cup did John guide West Ham to win in his first full season in charge?

865. What was West Ham's biggest win under the management of John?

866. In what year did John guide West Ham to the European Cup-Winners' Cup final, losing 4-2?

867. Which team did West Ham play in John's first game in charge at West Ham?

868. What East Anglian side did John manage later in his managerial career?

869. How many appearances did John make for West Ham between 1960 and 1963 (in all comps)?

870. Against which London club did John make his West Ham debut against in February 1960?

SCOTT PARKER

871. What is Scott's middle name – Martin, Matthew or Marcus?

872. At which London club did Scott start his professional football career, making his League debut in 1997?

873. How much did West Ham United pay for Scott in June 2007?

874. True or false: Scott was voted supporters player of the year at the end of the 2008/20009 season?

875. Against which club did Scott score his first Hammers goal in the 90th minute in a 2-1 away win during December 2007?

876. From which club did Scott sign when he joined West Ham United?

877. In which year was Scott born – 1979,1980 or 1981?

878. For which London team did Scott play between January 2004 and June 2005?

879. Which team were West Ham playing when Scott was sent-off after 85 minutes during October 2009 in a 2-2 home draw in the Premier League?

880. Which squad number did Scott wear for The Hammers during the 2009/2010 season?

EUROPEAN CUP WINNERS' CUP WINNERS - 1965

881. Who did West Ham beat in the final?

882. West Ham beat their opponents 2-0. Who scored both the goals?

883. Where was the final played?

884. Who did West Ham play in the semi-final, beating them 3-2 on aggregate?

885. Who was West Ham's highest goalscorer in European competition, scoring four goals in this Cup run?

886. Who scored the three goals in the semi-final over the two legs?

887. Which team were West Ham playing when the opponents scored an own goal?

888. Who played in goal for West Ham in the final?

889. Can you name seven players from the starting eleven that played in the final?

890. Five players played in all nine European games for West Ham. Can you name them?

BRYAN 'POP' ROBSON

891.   From which team did West Ham sign Bryan?

892.   Bryan scored on his Hammers debut, against who?

893.   When Bryan left West Ham, who did he join?

894.   Bryan finished as West Ham's highest goalscorer during the 1978-1979 season. How many goals did he score?

895.   How many goals did Bryan score in his first season at Upton Park - 3, 13 or 23?

896.   Where was Bryan born - Glasgow, Newcastle or Sunderland?

897.   Can you name the season in which Bryan was "Hammer of the Year"?

898.   During the 1971-1972 season Bryan scored a hat-trick in the League Cup, against who?

899.   How many goals did Bryan score in his Hammers career?

900.   On 16 May 1977 West Ham beat Manchester United 4-2 on the last day of the season - how many of the four goals did Bryan score?

HARRY REDKNAPP

901. Where was Harry born - Leeds, London or Leicester?

902. What was Harry's nickname at West Ham?

903. Harry made his West Ham debut in 1965, against who?

904. In December 1966 Harry scored in a 3-0 League win, against who?

905. Harry scored two goals in the 1967-1968 season. Which two teams did he score against?

906. How many appearances (in all comps) did Harry make for West Ham?

907. How many goals did Harry score for the Hammers (in all comps)?

908. During Harry's first season at West Ham he played seven League games, scoring one goal. Who did he score against?

909. Harry was best man to which West Ham teammate in 1967?

910. When Harry left West Ham in 1972, who did he sign for?

LEAGUE CUP FINALISTS - 1981

911.   Who did West Ham play in the League Cup final?

912.   West Ham's goalscorer scored from the penalty spot. Who was he?

913.   Who scored the goal for the opponents?

914.   Which opponent midfielder punched the ball over his goal to give West Ham the penalty?

915.   Who refereed the match?

916.   What was the score in the replay?

917.   Who scored West Ham's goal in the replay?

918.   At what stadium was the League Cup final replay played?

919.   Who scored for the opponents in the replay?

920.   Can you name two of the five teams that West Ham beat to reach the 1981 League Cup final?

RONNIE BOYCE

921. Where was Ronnie born in 1943 - London, Glasow or Birmingham?

922. What was Ronnie's nickname?

923. Ronnie made his Hammers debut in 1960, against who?

924. Who did Ronnie score his first West Ham goal against in 1961?

925. Ronnie scored the winner in the FA Cup final in 1964 in a 3-2 win over Preston North End. Who scored the other two?

926. Ronnie scored one European goal in his West Ham career. Who was that against?

927. In March 1970 Ronnie scored from the halfway line in a 5-1 win, against who?

928. In what year did Ronnie take charge of one game as West Ham's caretaker manager?

929. Against which club did Ronnie play against in his last League appearance for the Hammers?

930. In 1972 Ronnie had his testimonial match, against who?

IAN BISHOP

931. Where was Ian born - London, Leeds or Liverpool?

932. How many England 'B' caps did Ian win?

933. Where did West Ham sign Ian from?

934. Ian made his West Ham debut in 1989, against who?

935. In the 1989-1990 season Ian scored two League goals. Which two clubs were they against?

936. Ian scored his first Premier League goal for West Ham in a 3-2 defeat during the 1993-1994 season. Who were the opponents?

937. During the 1990-1991 season Ian scored two goals in the FA Cup run. Which two clubs were they against?

938. West Ham beat which East Anglian side 4-0 in April 1992, with Ian scoring one of the goals?

939. In how many of West Ham's 42 Premier League games did Ian play during the 1994-1995 season - 29, 31 or 33?

940. When Ian left Upton Park, which club did he join?

FA CUP FINALISTS - 2006

941. Who did West Ham play in the FA Cup final?

942. What was the score in the game?

943. Which West Ham players scored in this game?

944. At what stadium was the final played?

945. Which manager guided West Ham to the final?

946. Who played in goal for the Hammers?

947. Who scored the goal when West Ham beat Middlesbrough 1-0 in the FA Cup semi-final?

948. Can you name the team that West Ham beat 2-1 in the quarter-final, with Dean Ashton scoring twice?

949. Which East-Anglian side did West Ham beat 2-1 in the 3rd round?

950. Which midfielder scored twice for the opponents in the FA Cup Final?

JOHN MONCUR

951. In what year was John born - 1962, 1964 or 1966?

952. Where did John sign from to join West Ham?

953. John joined the Hammers in the summer of 1994. How much did he cost?

954. What was John's nickname at Upton Park?

955. John made his West Ham debut in August 1994, against who?

956. Who was John's first goal for West Ham against in October 1994?

957. For which club did John play four games for while on loan in 1986?

958. For which East Anglian side did John play (on loan) during his career?

959. During the 1997-1998 season John scored one Premier League goal in a 6-0 win, against who?

960. John scored one Premier League goal during the 1999-2000 season in a match against Bradford City in a nine-goal thriller. What was the score?

MANAGER: RON GREENWOOD

961. In which year did Ron take over as West Ham boss?

962. To what position did Ron guide West Ham in the League in his first season in charge?

963. What was the first Cup that Ron won as manager of West Ham?

964. Whp did Ron take over from as West Ham manager?

965. What was West Ham's biggest win under the management of Ron?

966. Who was appointed Ron's assistant manager in September 1970?

967. Ron guided West Ham to European Cup Winners' Cup glory in 1965. Who did they play?

968. What was Ron's last season in charge at Upton Park?

969. Ron guided West Ham to FA Cup success in 1975. Which London club did they play and beat 2-0?

970. Which manager replaced Ron as Hammers boss?

EUROPEAN CUP WINNERS' CUP FINALISTS - 1976

971. Who did West Ham play in the final?

972. Which West Ham players scored in the final?

973. What was the score in the final?

974. Where was the final played and in which stadium?

975. Which German club did the Hammers beat 4-3 on aggregate to reach the final?

976. Which West Ham player scored four European goals during this Cup run?

977. Which Hammers manager guided West Ham to this Cup Final success?

978. Which player was captain of West Ham for this final?

979. Who played in goal for the Hammers in all nine European games?

980. Can you name three of the four teams that West Ham beat to reach the final?

WEST HAM IN THE EUROPEAN CUP WINNERS' CUP

981. Which team knocked West Ham out of the 1980-1981 Cup run, losing 4-2 on aggregate?

982. Who scored six European goals in the 1980-1981 Cup run?

983. Who played in goal for all six European matches during 1980-1981?

984. What two players both scored three goals in West Ham's Cup run during 1965-1966?

985. Who was West Ham's manager during the 1965-1966 European Cup run?

986. Which club did West Ham lose to 5-2 on aggregate in the semi-final during the 1965-1966 Cup run?

987. Following on from question 986, which two players scored West Ham's goals?

988. Can you name the team that West Ham played in the 2nd round, winning 6-2 on aggregate during 1965-1966?

989. Can you name the team that West Ham played in the 3rd round, winning 2-1 on aggregate during 1965-1966?

990. Can you name five West Ham players that scored in the European Competition during 1965-1966?

WEST HAM UNITED - POT LUCK

991. Who was West Ham's highest goalscorer during the 2000-2001 season, scoring 11 Premier League and 3 FA Cup goals?

992. In what season was Mike Small top goalscorer with 13 League, 1 FA Cup and 4 League Cup goals?

993. Where did West Ham sign Peter Brabrook from?

994. During what season did Ron Greenwood take over as manager from Ted Fenton?

995. Can you name the five goalkeepers that appeared for the Hammers during the 1999-2000 season?

996. Which two players scored a total of 39 goals between them during the 1986-1987 season?

997. Who did West Ham play in the Charity Shield in 1975, losing 2-0 at Wembley?

998. From which club did West Ham sign Billy Jennings?

999. Who managed West Ham during the 2001-2002 season?

1000. Where did West Ham sign Dale Gordon from?

ANSWERS

BOBBY MOORE

1. 1941
2. Martin Peters and Geoff Hurst
3. 108
4. 1958
5. West Ham United (Playing for Fulham)
6. Manchester United
7. 17
8. Fulham
9. 1973
10. Southend United

TREVOR BROOKING

11. 1948
12. Burnley
13. 5
14. Arsenal
15. Hadleigh
16. 528
17. 1984
18. 47
19. 5
20. Portugal (April 1974)

WEST HAM IN THE LEAGUE CUP

21. John Sissons and Geoff Hurst
22. Liverpool
23. Charlton Athletic and Tottenham Hotspur
24. Frank Lampard
25. Bury
26. David Cross
27. Aston Villa and Walsall
28. Birmingham City and Aston Villa
29. Preston North End

30.   Geoff Hurst

SQUAD NUMBERS 2009-2010
31.	Kieron Dyer	7
32.	Mark Noble	16
33.	Carlton Cole	12
34.	Scott Parker	8
35.	Oliver Lee	34
36.	Jack Collison	31
37.	Matthew Upson	15
38.	Robert Green	1
39.	Luis Jimenez	17
40.	Radoslav Kovac	14

PLAYER OF THE YEAR
41.	2003-2004	Matthew Etherington
42.	2001-2002	Sebastien Schemmel
43.	1999-2000	Paulo Di Canio
44.	1997-1998	Rio Ferdinand
45.	1995-1996	Julian Dicks
46.	1993-1994	Trevor Morley
47.	1991-1992	Julian Dicks
48.	1989-1990	Julian Dicks
49.	1987-1988	Stewart Robson
50.	1985-1986	Tony Cottee

POSITIONS IN THE LEAGUE
51.	2005-2006	9th in the Premier League
52.	2001-2002	7th in the Premier League
53.	2000-2001	15th in the Premier League
54.	1995-1996	10th in the Premier League
55.	1991-1992	22nd in Division One
56.	1987-1988	16th in Division One
57.	1981-1982	9th in Division One

58.	1979-1980	7th in Division Two
59.	1972-1973	6th in Division One
60.	1965-1966	12th in Division One

JULIAN DICKS

61. 1968
62. Birmingham City
63. 4
64. Chelsea
65. The Terminator
66. John Lyall
67. 4
68. Athletic Bilbao
69. David Burrows and Mike Marsh
70. Ipswich Town

ALAN DEVONSHIRE

71. 1956
72. West Bromwich Albion
73. Watford
74. 1978-1979
75. West Bromwich Albion (2 goals) and Norwich City
76. Ron Greenwood
77. £5,000
78. Everton
79. Northern Ireland
80. 10

TONY COTTEE

81. 7
82. 1965
83. 1986
84. TC
85. Selangor

86. £2.05 million (£2 million and £50,000)
87. Tottenham Hotspur
88. Sweden (in 1986)
89. 5
90. Millwall

TOMMY TAYLOR

91. 1951
92. Leyton Orient
93. Peter Bennett
94. 13
95. 340
96. Southampton
97. Clyde Best, Billy Bonds and Bryan 'Pop' Robson
98. Chelsea
99. 8
100. Leyton Orient

MANAGER: GIANFRANCO ZOLA

101. 1966
102. 10
103. Manuel Da Costa
104. 2008
105. 9th (2008/2009 season)
106. Alan Curbishley
107. Sunderland (during November 2008)
108. True
109. Chelsea
110. Diego Tristan

POSITIONS IN THE LEAGUE

111. 2002-2003   18th in the Premier League
112. 1997-1998   8th in the Premier League
113. 1996-1997   14th in the Premier League

114.	1993-1994	13th in the Premier League
115.	1988-1989	19th in Division One
116.	1984-1985	16th in Division One
117.	1977-1978	20th in Division One
118.	1975-1976	18th in Division One
119.	1968-1969	8th in Division One
120.	1951-1952	12th in Division Two

2008-2009

121.	Craig Bellamy
122.	Wigan Athletic
123.	14
124.	Diego Tristan
125.	Carlton Cole
126.	Robert Green
127.	Craig Bellamy
128.	Stoke City
129.	Middlesbrough
130.	David Di Michele

PLAYERS NATIONALITIES

131.	James Collins	Wales
132.	Paolo Di Canio	Italy
133.	Julien Faubert	France
134.	Tomas Repka	Czech Republic
135.	Javier Mascherano	Argentina
136.	Trevor Brooking	England
137.	Slaven Bilic	Croatia
138.	Yossi Benayoun	Israel
139.	Scott Parker	England
140.	Stan Lazaridis	Australia

PLAYERS' TRANSFERS: WHERE DID THEY COME FROM?

| 141. | Nolberto Solano | Newcastle United |

142.	Paolo Di Canio	Sheffield Wednesday
143.	Carlos Tevez	Corinthians
144.	Roy Carroll	Manchester United
145.	Christian Dailly	Blackburn Rovers
146.	Matthew Etherington	Tottenham Hotspur
147.	John Hartson	Arsenal
148.	Dean Ashton	Norwich City
149.	Mike Marsh	Liverpool
150.	Neil Ruddock	Liverpool

MANAGER: BILLY BONDS

151. West Ham's Youth Team
152. 1990
153. 13th
154. Oldham Athletic
155. Lou Macari
156. Tim Breaker and Iain Dowie
157. Bournemouth
158. Southampton
159. 1993-1994
160. Harry Redknapp

MARLON HAREWOOD

161. Nottingham Forest
162. Wimbledon
163. 1-1
164. Ipswich Town
165. 1979
166. Crewe Alexandra
167. Walsall
168. Millwall
169. Southend United
170. Aston Villa

RIO FERDINAND

171.   London
172.   Central Defence
173.   Sheffield Wednesday
174.   1998 (against Cameroon)
175.   £18 million
176.   £30 million
177.   1997-1998
178.   Blackburn Rovers and Coventry City
179.   35
180.   The Intertoto Cup

PLAY-OFF FINAL WINNERS 2005

181.   Preston North End
182.   Bobby Zamora
183.   The Millennium Stadium (Cardiff)
184.   Stephen Bywater, Mark Noble and Christian Dailly
185.   James Walker and Stephen Bywater
186.   Teddy Sheringham and Carl Fletcher
187.   Bobby Zamora and Marlon Harewood
188.   Mike Riley
189.   Billy Davies
190.   Alan Pardew

WEST HAM UNITED - 1980s

191.   Paul Goddard
192.   41 years old
193.   Leroy Rosenior
194.   Ray Stewart
195.   Tony Cottee
196.   Alvin Martin
197.   Francois Van der Elst
198.   28
199.   3rd in Division One

200. 4-0 against Tottenham Hotspur

JOE COLE
201. 1981
202. Harry Redknapp
203. Manchester United
204. Birmingham City
205. Coventry City, Bradford City, Coventry City, Derby County
       and Southampton
206. 2002-2003
207. Jermain Defoe
208. 5th
209. 2003
210. Chelsea

MARTIN PETERS
211. 1943
212. Midfield
213. Ron Greenwood
214. 1966
215. 1
216. £200,000
217. Jimmy Greaves
218. Cardiff City
219. League Cup Final
220. Norwich City

LIAM BRADY
221. 1956
222. 1987
223. Ascoli, Italy
224. Norwich City
225. Arsenal
226. 2

227. Manchester United
228. Luton Town and Derby County
229. Republic of Ireland
230. 72

PLAYERS PLAYING FOR THEIR COUNTRY

231. Trevor Brooking (England)   47 Caps
232. Phil Parkes (England)   1 Cap
233. Martin Peters (England)   67 Caps
234. Ken Brown (England)   1 Cap
235. Tony Cottee (Engalnd)   7 Caps
236. Alan Devonshire (England)   8 Caps
237. Geoff Hurst (England)   49 Caps
238. Frank Lampard, SR (England)   2 Caps
239. Alvin Martin (England)   17 Caps
240. Bobby Moore (England)   108 Caps

LEAGUE GOALSCORERS FOR THE HAMMERS

241. Steve Whitton   6
242. David Kelly   7
243. Ted Fenton   27
244. James Ruffell   159
245. Bobby Gould   15
246. Frank McAvennie   49
247. Pat Holland   23
248. Clive Allen   17
249. Graham Paddon   11
250. Stuart Slater   11

FRANK McAVENNIE

251. Glasgow
252. Birmingham City
253. Queens Park Rangers
254. St. Mirren

255. 26 goals
256. Celtic
257. £1.25 million
258. Nottingham Forest
259. 6 goals
260. Australia

MANAGER: HARRY REDKNAPP

261. 1987
262. Intertoto Cup
263. 2004
264. Graham Rix
265. 1992
266. 1994
267. Jim Smith
268. 1999
269. 13 games
270. 1994-1995

CLYDE BEST

271. Bermudan
272. Trinidad and Tobago
273. Arsenal
274. 5
275. 47
276. John Charles
277. 1971-1972
278. Feyenoord
279. Tampa Bay Rowdies
280. Sheffield United

LEAGUE GOALSCORERS FOR THE HAMMERS

281. Billy Bonds   48 goals
282. Trevor Brooking   88 goals

283.	Geoff Hurst	180 goals
284.	Malcolm Allison	10 goals
285.	Len Goulden	54 goals
286.	Alvin Martin	27 goals
287.	Joe Cockcroft	3 goals
288.	Bryan 'Pop' Robson	94 goals
289.	Ray Stewart	62 goals
290.	Albert Cadwell	1 goal

TONY GALE

291.	Keith Hackett
292.	London
293.	300
294.	5
295.	Fulham
296.	1984-1985
297.	Galey
298.	Bobby Campbell
299.	John Lyall
300.	Republic of Ireland XI

PLAYERS' LEAGUE APPERANCES FOR WEST HAM

301.	Geoff Hurst	410 (1)
302.	John Sissons	210 (3)
303.	Richard Walker	292
304.	Stan Earle	258
305.	Pat Holland	227 (18)
306.	Julian Dicks	262
307.	Tony Gale	293 (7)
308.	Paul Goddard	159 (11)
309.	George Parris	211 (28)
310.	Bobby Moore	543 (1)

STUART PEARCE

311. Manchester City, West Ham United, Newcastle United, Nottingham Forest, Coventry City
312. 4
313. 1998
314. Tottenham Hotspur
315. 1-0 to West Ham United
316. 0
317. Newcastle United
318. Arsenal and Southampton
319. Tottenham Hotspur (in a 3-2 defeat)
320. Manchester City

PLAYERS' LEAGUE APPEARANCES FOR WEST HAM

321.	Fred Blackburn	217
322.	Tommy Yews	346
323.	John Bond	381
324.	Jimmy Ruffell	505
325.	Phil Parkes	344
326.	George Kay	237
327.	Martin Peters	302
328.	Peter Brabrook	167
329.	Tommy Taylor	340
330.	Joe Cockcroft	251

PAUL INCE

331. London
332. Captain England
333. Newcastle United
334. Manchester United
335. Spain
336. FA Cup
337. The Guv'nor
338. Inter Milan

339. 53
340. Middlesbrough

PAOLO DI CANIO

341. Italian
342. 1968
343. Celtic
344. Sheffield Wednesday
345. Paul Alcock
346. 1999
347. Wimbledon
348. FIFA Fair Play Award
349. Charlton Athletic
350. Lazio

STEVE POTTS

351. Pottsy
352. 1983
353. 1
354. USA
355. Queens Park Rangers
356. 1992-1993 and 1994-1995
357. Hull City
358. Ludek Miklosko and Kevin Keen
359. John Lyall
360. Play in all 42 Premier League matches

FA CUP WINNERS - 1975

361. Fulham
362. 2-0
363. Alan Taylor
364. Rochdale
365. 13
366. Mervyn Day

367. *1*
368. *Pat Partridge*
369. *Ron Greenwood*
370. *Bobby Moore and Alan Mullery*

PAUL GODDARD

371. *1959*
372. *John Lyall*
373. *Queens Park Rangers*
374. *Liverpool*
375. *170*
376. *54*
377. *Everton*
378. *Newcastle United*
379. *Ipswich Town*
380. *Iceland*

GEOFF HURST

381. *Score a hat-trick in 1966*
382. *24*
383. *1976*
384. *Essex*
385. *1998*
386. *Stoke City*
387. *1972*
388. *180*
389. *411*
390. *Wolverhampton Wanderers*

MANAGER: ALAN PARDEW

391. *2003*
392. *Tommy Burns*
393. *Trevor Brooking*
394. *1961*

395. *Charlton Athletic*
396. *Hayden Mullins*
397. *Blackburn Rovers (August 2005) in a 3-1 win*
398. *Liverpool*
399. *Crystal Palace*
400. *Charlton Athletic*

DAVID CROSS
401. *1950*
402. *West Bromwich Albion*
403. *£180,000*
404. *West Bromwich Albion*
405. *Psycho*
406. *Norwich City*
407. *18*
408. *Wolverhampton Wanderers*
409. *Grimsby Town and Tottenham Hotspur*
410. *77*

ALAN CURBISHLEY
411. *1973*
412. *Birmingham City and Aston Villa*
413. *Alan Pardew*
414. *Steve Gritt*
415. *2000*
416. *Chelsea*
417. *Birmingham City*
418. *Manchester United (1-0)*
419. *85*
420. *11*

CHRISTIAN DAILLY
421. *Scottish*
422. *Blackburn Rovers*

423. Dundee
424. 34
425. Dundee United
426. Craig Brown
427. Malta
428. 2000-2001
429. Harry Redknapp
430. Play in all 38 Premier League matches

DAVID JAMES
431. 1970
432. Watford
433. Graeme Souness
434. Aston Villa
435. 2001
436. Manchester City
437. Mexico
438. Watford
439. 26
440. Glenn Roeder

BILLY BONDS
441. London
442. Charlton Athletic
443. Bobby Moore
444. Lift the FA Cup twice
445. Bonzo
446. 59
447. Chelsea
448. 1988
449. 793
450. Southampton

WHAT WAS THE SCORE?

451. **Charlton Athletic**
     Premier League, December 2000   5-0 win
452. **Leeds United**
     League Cup, November 1966   7-0 win
453. **Bristol City**
     League Cup, October 1984   6-1 win
454. **Fulham**
     Division 1, February 1968   7-2 win
455. **Tottenham Hotspur**
     Premier League, April 1994   4-1 win
456. **Norwich City**
     Division 1, April 1991   4-0 win
457. **Coventry City**
     Division 1, November 1981   5-2 win
458. **Aldershot**
     FA Cup, January 1991   6-1 win
459. **Ararat Erevan**
     European Cup Winners' Cup, November 1975   3-1 win
460. **Charlton Athletic**
     Premier League, November 2001   4-4 draw

HAT-TRICK HEROES

461. **Stoke City**
     November 1957, 5-0 win, Division 2

                                             Vic Keeble
462. **West Bromwich Albion**
     August 1968, 4-0 win, Division 1

                                             Martin Peters
463. **Leicester City**
     December 1967, 4-2 win, Division 1

                                             Brian Dear
464. **Coventry City**
     September 1983, 5-2 win, Division 1

465.   **Sheffield United**
       March 1990, 5-0 win, Division 2

Jimmy Quinn

466.   **West Bromwich Albion**
       March 1959, 3-1 win, Division 1

Johnny Dick

467.   **Sheffield Wednesday**
       May 1997, 5-1 win, Premier League

Paul Kitson

468.   **Stoke City**
       December 1975, 3-1 win, Division 1

Billy Jennings

469.   **Notts County**
       December 1982, 3-3 draw, League Cup

Francois Van der Elst

470.   **Port Vale**
       January 1985, 4-1 win, FA Cup

Paul Goddard

MATTHEW ETHERINGTON

471.   **1981**
472.   **Tottenham Hotspur**
473.   **2003**
474.   **Bradford City**
475.   **2003-2004**
476.   **Teddy Sheringham and Nigel Reo-Coker**
477.   **Wimbledon**
478.   **Ipswich Town**
479.   **11**
480.   **Glenn Roeder**

CRAIG FORREST

481.   **Canada**

482. *Ipswich Town*
483. *1997*
484. *56*
485. *Concacaf Gold Cup*
486. *8th*
487. *The Intertoto Cup (1 appearance)*
488. *Harry Redknapp*
489. *Stephen Bywater, Ian Feuer, Shaka Hislop and Sasa Ilic*
490. *Shaka Hislop*

CLIVE ALLEN
491. *1961*
492. *Centre forward*
493. *Chelsea*
494. *Chelsea*
495. *Tottenham Hotspur*
496. *Millwall*
497. *18*
498. *Brazil*
499. *West Bromwich Albion*
500. *Luton Town*

LEAGUE CUP FINALISTS - 1966
501. *West Bromwich Albion*
502. *Cardiff City*
503. *Geoff Hurst and Martin Peters*
504. *Geoff Hurst*
505. *2-1 v. West Bromwich Albion*
506. *1-4 v. West Bromwich Albion*
507. *Ron Greenwood*
508. *Bobby Moore*
509. *Bobby Moore, Johnny Byrne and Martin Peters*
510. *Geoff Hurst*

JOHNNY BYRNE
511. 1939
512. Crystal Palace
513. Budgie
514. 1963-1964
515. Cardiff City
516. Sheffield Wednesday
517. Sunderland
518. 1964-1965
519. Tottenham Hotspur
520. Crystal Palace

CARLTON COLE
521. 1983
522. Chelsea
523. 12
524. Alan Pardew
525. Arsenal
526. True: against Charlton Athletic during August 2006)
527. Derby County
528. Bobby Zamora
529. Fabio Capello
530. Aston Villa

ALAN DICKENS
531. London
532. 1981
533. Dicho
534. Notts County
535. 192
536. 23
537. Chelsea
538. 2
539. Tottenham Hotspur

540.   Colchester United

TOMAS REPKA
541.   Fiorentina
542.   2
543.   Glenn Roeder
544.   Banik Ostrava
545.   2001-2002
546.   £5.5 million
547.   31
548.   Czech Republic
549.   Faroe Islands
550.   2

PHIL PARKES
551.   Queens Park Rangers
552.   John Lyall
553.   £565,000
554.   344
555.   Parkesy
556.   Oldham Athletic
557.   1980-1981
558.   Ipswich Town
559.   Bobby Ferguson and Mervyn Day
560.   Oldham Athletic

ALVIN MARTIN
561.   Liverpool
562.   Billy Bonds
563.   Stretch
564.   17
565.   Ron Greenwood
566.   1976
567.   Aston Villa

568. Martin Thomas, Chris Hedworth and Peter Beardsley
569. Oldham Athletic and Newcastle United
570. Leyton Orient

FRANK LAMPARD (SNR)
571. London
572. 1967
573. Yugoslavia
574. 2
575. Southend United
576. Harry Redknapp
577. Manchester City
578. Liverpool
579. 551
580. Everton

WEST HAM UNITED - POT LUCK
581. 1895
582. 1904
583. 1900
584. 1993-1994
585. Claret and Blue
586. East London
587. Tottenham Hotspur
588. 3rd in old Division One
589. Sunderland
590. 5-1

TIM BREAKER
591. 1965
592. 2
593. Luton Town
594. Billy Bonds
595. Swindon Town

596.   Plymouth Argyle
597.   33
598.   Coventry City, Everton and Newcastle United
599.   Queens Park Rangers
600.   8

MANAGER: LOU MACARI

601.   Edinburgh
602.   Celtic
603.   West Ham United
604.   Liverpool
605.   1989
606.   5
607.   Celtic
608.   24
609.   Stoke City
610.   Billy Bonds

FREDERIC KANOUTE

611.   Lyon
612.   2
613.   Wimbledon and Coventry City
614.   Charlton Athletic
615.   14 goals (11 League and 3 FA Cup)
616.   Mali
617.   Chelsea
618.   Walsall
619.   2003
620.   Seville

WEST HAM UNITED - POT LUCK

621.   Christian Dailly
622.   Leicester City
623.   For attending a night club the day before a match

624. Tottenham Hotspur
625. 13
626. NK Osijek and Steaua Bucharest
627. Tottenham Hotspur
628. Florin Raducioiu
629. Syd King
630. Benfica

MERVYN DAY

631. 1955
632. 1973
633. Ipswich Town
634. Bobby Ferguson
635. Sunderland
636. Leyton Orient
637. PFA Young Player of the Year award
638. Fulham
639. Aston Villa
640. Charlton Athletic

2004-2005 RESULTS IN THE CHAMPIONSHIP

641. v. Plymouth Argyle (H)   Won 5-0
642. v. Nottingham Forest (H)   Won 3-2
643. v. Cardiff City (A)   Lost 4-1
644. v. Ipswich Town (H)   Drew 1-1
645. v. Brighton & Hove Albion (A)   Drew 2-2
646. v. Sunderland (A)   Won 2-0
647. v. Leicester City (A)   Drew 0-0
648. v. Watford (H)   Won 3-2
649. v. Watford (A)   Won 2-1
650. v. Leeds United (A)   Lost 2-1

MARK WARD

651. Liverpool

652. Oldham Athletic
653. £250,000
654. Birmingham City
655. 3 goals
656. Ian Bishop and Trevor Morley
657. Everton
658. Howard Kendall
659. Birmingham City
660. Midfield

JOE KIRKUP

661. 1939
662. Manchester City
663. Leicester City
664. 11
665. 6 goals
666. Ipswich Town
667. 187
668. £27,000
669. South Africa
670. Chelsea

PLAYERS' TRANSFERS: WHERE DID THEY GO?

671.	Carl Fletcher	Crystal Palace
672.	Clyde Best	Tampa Bay Rowdies
673.	Lee Chapman	Ipswich Town
674.	Stewart Robson	Coventry City
675.	Slaven Bilic	Everton
676.	David Cross	Manchester City
677.	Bobby Moore	Fulham
678.	George Parris	Birmingham City
679.	Kevin Lock	Fulham
680.	Mervyn Day	Leyton Orient

JERMAIN DEFOE

681. 1982
682. Bournemouth
683. Walsall
684. 10
685. Cardiff City
686. 9
687. Sweden
688. Tottenham Hotspur
689. Bobby Zamora
690. Poland

WEST HAM UNITED - 1960s

691. Martin Peters, Joe Kirkup, Ronnie Boyce and Tony Scott
692. Geoff Hurst
693. Brian Dear
694. Ted Fenton and Ron Greenwood
695. 19
696. 2-2
697. Geoff Hurst and Johnny Byrne
698. Geoff Hurst
699. 5-3 to West Ham United
700. Ronnie Boyce

RAY STEWART

701. 1959
702. Right back
703. 20
704. Preston North End
705. Dundee United
706. 62
707. Tonka
708. Wales
709. 10

710.   St. Johnstone

FA CUP WINNERS - 1964
711.   Preston North End
712.   3-2
713.   Charlton Athletic and Leyton Orient
714.   Manchester United
715.   Boyce (two goals) and Geoff Hurst (one goal)
716.   Hillsborough
717.   Geoff Hurst
718.   Jim Standen
719.   May (2nd)
720.   John Sissons, Geoff Hurst and Ronnie Boyce

NEIL ORR
721.   1959
722.   Greenock Morton
723.   £400,000
724.   Manchester United
725.   Bury
726.   33 starts
727.   St. Mirren
728.   7 caps
729.   West Bromwich Albion and Newcastle United
730.   Hibernian

MANAGER: GLENN ROEDER
731.   Gillingham and Watford
732.   7th in the Premier League
733.   Harry Redknapp
734.   15
735.   Ludek Miklosko
736.   Paul Goddard
737.   Tomas Repka

738. Jermain Defoe and Frederic Kanoute
739. Leyton Orient, Queens Park Rangers, Newcastle United and Watford
740. Newcastle United

IAIN DOWIE
741. Oldham Athletic
742. Queens Park Rangers
743. Billy Bonds
744. Hull City
745. Luton Town
746. 4 goals
747. Harry Redknapp
748. 9 goals
749. Manchester City
750. Nottingham Forest

GEORGE PARRIS
751. 1981
752. Liverpool
753. Smokey
754. West Bromwich Albion
755. Leyton Orient
756. 8 (5 League and 3 FA Cup)
757. 17 (12 League, 4 FA Cup and 1 League Cup)
758. Ludek Miklosko
759. 239
760. Birmingham City

MICHAEL CARRICK
761. Coventry City
762. Intertoto Cup
763. Bradford City
764. Aston Villa

765. 1981

766. Mexico

767. Blackburn Rovers and Chelsea

768. Birmingham City

769. 2003-2004

770. Tottenham Hotspur

FA CUP WINNERS - 1980

771. Arsenal

772. 1-0

773. Trevor Brooking

774. 13th minute

775. John Lyall

776. Phil Parkes

777. Paul Allen

778. Leyton Orient

779. Ray Stewart (2 against Leyton Orient and 1 against Aston Villa)

780. Everton

FRANK LAMPARD (JNR)

781. 1978

782. Swansea City

783. Coventry City

784. Barnsley

785. 19

786. Walsall

787. Play in all 38 Premier League matches

788. NK Osijek

789. 3

790. Austria

PAT HOLLAND

791. London

792. Bournemouth
793. Patsy
794. Liverpool
795. 1980-1981
796. Tottenham Hotspur
797. Manchester United and Newcastle United
798. 23 goals
799. Tottenham Hotspur
800. Leyton Orient

WEST HAM UNITED - 1970s
801. Jimmy Greaves
802. Scotland
803. 6-0
804. David Cross
805. 4-1 v. Southampton in Division One
806. Clyde Best
807. Clyde Best, Billy Bonds, Bryan 'Pop' Robson and Tommy Taylor
808. Tommy Taylor
809. Football League Division Two
810. Geoff Hurst

WEST HAM UNITED - POT LUCK
811. I'm Forever Blowing Bubbles
812. Charlton Athletic
813. Alvin Martin
814. Blackburn Rovers
815. David Speedie
816. Chris Hughton
817. AC Milan
818. Phil Parkes and Geoff Pike
819. Arsenal
820. Lyon

WEST HAM IN THE FA CUP

821. Wrexham
822. Manchester United
823. Macclesfield Town and Chelsea
824. Villa Park
825. Samassi Abou
826. Southend United
827. West Bromwich Albion and Aston Villa
828. Chelsea
829. Arsenal and Charlton Athletic
830. Alan Devonshire, Phil Parkes, Stuart Pearson and Ray Stewart

DON HUTCHISON

831. 1971
832. Newcastle United
833. Liverpool
834. Hutch
835. Harry Redknapp
836. Tottenham Hotspur and Chelsea
837. Sheffield United
838. Glenn Roeder
839. Newcastle United
840. 9

WEST HAM UNITED - 1990s

841. Trevor Morley
842. Ian Bishop and Julian Dicks
843. Tony Cottee
844. Julian Dicks
845. Paul Kitson
846. Ian Wright
847. Frank Lampard
848. The Intertoto Cup

849. John Hartson
850. Ludek Miklosko

WEST HAM IN CUP COMPETITIONS

851.	FA Cup Finalists	2006
852.	League Cup Finalists	1981
853.	FA Cup Winners	1980
854.	European Cup Winners' Cup Finalists	1976
855.	FA Cup Winners	1975
856.	League Cup Finalists	1966
857.	European Cup Winners' Cup Winners	1965
858.	FA Cup Winners	1964
859.	FA Cup Finalists	1923
860.	FA Cup Semi-Finalists	1991

MANAGER: JOHN LYALL

861. 1974
862. Ron Greenwood
863. 13th
864. FA Cup
865. 10-0 v. Bury in the League Cup in October 1983
866. 1976
867. Manchester City
868. Ipswich Town
869. 34 (30 League, 2 FA Cup and 2 League Cup)
870. Chelsea

SCOTT PARKER

871. Matthew
872. Charlton Athletic
873. £7 million
874. True
875. Middlesbrough
876. Newcastle United

877. 1980
878. Chelsea
879. Arsenal
880. 8

EUROPEAN CUP WINNERS' CUP WINNERS - 1965

881. TSV Munich 1860
882. Alan Sealey
883. Wembley
884. Real Zaragoza
885. Brian Dear
886. Brian Dear, Johnny Byrne and John Sissons
887. Lausanne
888. Jim Standen
889. Jim Standen, Joe Kirkup, Jack Birkett, Martin Peters, Ken Brown, Bobby Moore, Alan Sealey, Ronnie Boyce, Geoff Hurst, Brian Dear and John Sissons
890. Ronnie Boyce, Ken Brown, Geoff Hurst, Martin Peters and John Sissons

BRYAN 'POP' ROBSON

891. Newcastle United
892. Nottingham Forest
893. Sunderland
894. 28 Division 1 goals
895. 3
896. Sunderland
897. 1972-1973
898. Sheffield United (in a 5-0 win)
899. 104
900. 2 goals

HARRY REDKNAPP

901. London

902. 'Arry-boy
903. Sunderland
904. West Bromwich Albion
905. Burnley and Sunderland
906. 175
907. 8
908. Tottenham Hotspur
909. Billy Bonds
910. Bournemouth

LEAGUE CUP FINALISTS - 1981
911. Liverpool
912. Ray Stewart
913. Alan Kennedy
914. Terry McDermott
915. Clive Thomas
916. 2-1 to Liverpool
917. Paul Goddard
918. Villa Park
919. Kenny Dalglish and Alan Hansen (deflected off Billy Bonds)
920. Burnley, Charlton Athletic, Barnsley, Tottenham Hotspur and Coventry City

RONNIE BOYCE
921. London
922. Ticker
923. Preston North End
924. Blackpool (in a 2-2 draw)
925. John Sissons and Geoff Hurst
926. La Gantoise
927. Manchester City (at Maine Road)
928. 1990
929. Leicester City

930. Manchester United

IAN BISHOP
931. Liverpool
932. 1
933. Manchester City
934. Leicester City
935. West Bromwich Albion and Bournemouth
936. Sheffield United
937. Aldershot and Luton Town
938. Norwich City
939. 31
940. Manchester City

FA CUP FINALISTS - 2006
941. Liverpool
942. 3-3 (Liverpool won 3-1 on penalties)
943. Dean Ashton and Paul Konchesky (the other was an own-goal by Jamie Carragher)
944. The Millennium Stadium
945. Alan Pardew
946. Shaka Hislop
947. Marlon Harewood
948. Manchester City
949. Norwich City
950. Steven Gerrard

JOHN MONCUR
951. 1966
952. Swindon Town
953. £1 million
954. Moncs
955. Norwich City
956. Chelsea

957. Doncaster Rovers
958. Ipswich Town
959. Barnsley
960. Bradford City

MANAGER: RON GREENWOOD
961. 1961
962. 8th
963. The FA Cup in 1964
964. Ted Fenton
965. 8-0 win v. Sunderland in October 1968
966. John Lyall
967. TSV Munich 1860
968. 1973-1974
969. Fulham
970. John Lyall

EUROPEAN CUP WINNERS' CUP FINALISTS - 1976
971. Anderlecht
972. Pat Holland and Keith Robson
973. 4-2 to Anderlecht
974. Heysel Stadium, Brussels
975. Eintracht Frankfurt
976. Robson
977. John Lyall
978. Billy Bonds
979. Mervyn Day
980. Lahden Reipas, Ararat Erevan, Den Haag and Eintracht Frankfurt

WEST HAM IN THE EUROPEAN CUP WINNERS' CUP
981. Dynamo Tbilishi
982. David Cross
983. Phil Parkes

984. *Johnny Byrne and Martin Peters*
985. *Ron Greenwood*
986. *Borussia Dortmund*
987. *Martin Peters and Johnny Byrne*
988. *Olympiakos*
989. *FC Magdeburg*
990. *Geoff Hurst, Johnny Byrne, Martin Peters, Peter Brabrook and John Sissons*

WEST HAM UNITED - POT LUCK

991. *Frederic Kanoute*
992. *1991-1992*
993. *Chelsea*
994. *1960-1961*
995. *Stephen Bywater, Ian Feuer, Craig Forrest, Shaka Hislop, Sasa Ilic*
996. *Tony Cottee and Frank McAvennie*
997. *Derby County*
998. *Watford*
999. *Glenn Roeder*
1000. *Glasgow Rangers*

OTHER BOOKS BY CHRIS COWLIN:

The Cricket Quiz Book
Foreword by: Dickie Bird MBE
ISBN: 1-906358-00-1   978-1-906358-00-6
Price: £7.99

Did you know that cricket is the second most popular sport in the world and has been an established team sport for centuries, with more than 100 cricket-playing nations now recognised by the International Cricket Council? No doubt those questions haven't left cricket aficionados remotely stumped, but be prepared to be caught out by the 1,000 leg-breaking quiz questions in this book.

Your innings will require you to recall facts and figures relating to every possible aspect of the game of cricket from players to umpires and national to international matches, together with all kinds of trivia, so you could very easily find yourself in a real spin and may need to enlist the help of friends to bail you out before a sneaky Chinaman bowls you over, slips you up or reduces you to a pile of ashes.

Whether you find yourself top of the batting order or limping with a square leg, this book, with a fitting foreword by Dickie Bird, contains a wealth of knowledge about the sport that is guaranteed to enthral all cricket fans, and questions that will stimulate fond memories and friendly debates for many an entertaining hour.

The Gooners Quiz Book
Foreword by: Bob Wilson
ISBN: 1-904444-77-6   978-1-904444-77-0
Price: £8.99

Will you do the Gooners proud as you display an impressive knowledge of your favourite club, Arsenal, or will you instead prove yourself to be a complete goon, as trip over your own feet in search of the answers to the 1,000 cunning questions in this quiz book?

Covering every aspect of the club's history from players to managers and from national to international competitions since its foundation over a century ago, and with a fitting Foreword by former Scotland and Arsenal goalkeeping legend and TV presenter, Bob Wilson, this book will challenge Gooners fans of all ages as well as providing fascinating facts and figures both to enthral and to trigger fond memories and ardent discussions.

If you find yourself floundering, you can recover your dignity and find consolation in the fact that £1 from the sale of every book will go to the Willow Foundation, a charity founded by Bob and Megs Wilson and dedicated to arranging individually tailored 'Special Days' for seriously ill young adults.

OTHER BOOKS BY CHRIS COWLIN:

The Official Aston Villa Quiz Book
Foreword by: Graham Taylor OBE
ISBN: 1-906358-05-2   978-1-906358-05-1
Price: £7.99

Will you be a roaring lion or a quivering mouse as you attempt to face the villains of this book, i.e. the 1,000 challenging quiz questions that will have your minds hopping through over a hundred years of Aston Villa's history at lightning pace?

No stone remains unturned in terms of question topics, from cherished players, memorable managers and thrilling competitions to opponents, transfers, nationalities and awards, interspersed with sneaky bits of trivia to test the knowledge of even the most ardent Villa aficionado.

With a fitting foreword by Graham Taylor OBE, this book is a veritable mine of interesting facts and figures and is guaranteed to spark fond memories of much-loved characters and enthralling matches, and no doubt even heated discussion, as fans pit their wits against family and friends.

The Official Wolves Quiz Book
Foreword by: John Richards
ISBN: 1-904444-94-6   978-1-904444-94-7
Price: £7.99

You might think you know all there is to know about Wolves, but what if they're disguised in sheep's clothing and take the form of 1,000 tricky quiz questions that could give you a nasty bite? Your brains will certainly have to adopt the role of wanderer as you try to cast your minds back well over a century to the very beginning of the club's long history.

Questions cover every imaginable aspect of the club, from memorable managers and players, through transfer fees, opponents, scores and awards, to every competition you can think of, and they are sure to trigger vivid and treasured recollections of the colourful characters and nail-biting matches that have made the club what it is today.

With a fitting foreword by John Richards, this book is bursting at the seams with interesting facts and figures and is guaranteed to challenge even the most ardent fan as well as provide hours of entertainment for the whole family.

OTHER BOOKS BY CHRIS COWLIN:

The Official Carry On Quiz Book
Foreword by: Norman Hudis and Jacki Piper
ISBN: 1-904444-97-0   978-1-904444-97-8
Price: £7.99
Who can forget the cheeky humour, outrageous characters and slapstick comedy that have characterised the 'Carry On' films over the last fifty years? Well, don't lose your head if you discover that the 1,000 questions in this quiz book highlight a few holes in your memory and you end up in hospital screaming for the saucy nurse and ending up with the grumpy old matron!
Covering every aspect of the 'Carry On' genre – the movies, release dates, characters, the stars and their lives, debuts, and much more – this book will propel you on a whirlwind journey from the Wild West to the Khyber Pass and every conceivable location in between, hotfooting through a range of historical eras, and jumping between black-and-white and Technicolor worlds.
Even if you find you're cruising on rough waters, carry on regardless, make the most of the entertainment facilities, delve into the treasure trove of facts and figures, and allow your fond recollections to turn your frowns into the smiles and giggles that encapsulate the 'Carry On' ethos.

The Southend United Quiz Book
Foreword by: Frank Dudley
ISBN: 1-904444-91-1   978-1904444-91-6
Price: £5.99
Will you be a Shrimper with a record catch as you reel in the answers to the 800 tricky questions in this quiz book about Southend United Football Club, or will you be singing the Blues as you bemoan the one, or more, that got away?
Your knowledge about all aspects of the club since its formation will be tested to the limit, from memorable managers and players to transfer fees, opponents, scores, awards and all the unforgettable competitions and matches that have kept fans on the edge of their seats throughout the club's long history.
With a fitting foreword by Frank Dudley, this quiz book is brimming with interesting facts and figures and is guaranteed to provide hours of entertainment, reminiscing and discussion for fans of the club.

OTHER BOOKS BY CHRIS COWLIN:

Celebrities' Favourite Football Teams
Foreword by: Sir Alex Ferguson CBE
ISBN: 1-904444-84-9   978-1904444-84-8
Price: £6.99

We all like to delve into the minds and lives of our beloved celebrity figures, but this fascinating read is not celebrity gossip, it comes straight from the horse's mouth to reveal all you ever wanted to know about celebrities' favourite football teams and players.

With a fitting Foreword by footballing legend Sir Alex Ferguson CBE, this book is a must-read for football fans who wish to know which celebrity is a fellow aficionado of their club, or perhaps a supporter of 'the enemy', as well as for the rest of the population, who just love to know what makes our celebrities tick.

And it is also a must-buy, as all royalties from the sale of this book will be donated to The Willow Foundation, a charity set up by the legendary Bob Wilson and his wife Megs in 1999 to enable seriously ill young adults to enjoy the treat of a 'Special Day' with family and friends.

The Official Watford Football Club Quiz Book
Foreword by: Graham Taylor OBE
ISBN: 1-904444-85-7   978-1-904444-85-5
Price: £7.99

Be prepared to stir up a veritable hornets nest as you strive to meet the challenge of answering 1,000 testing questions about Watford Football Club. This quiz book certainly has the 'ouch' factor, guaranteeing that even the most ardent fan will get stung several times along the way.

Covering every subject imaginable about the Hornets, from players of old to the most recent Cup competitions, it not only contains a wealth of interesting facts and figures but also will stir up fond memories of all the great personalities and nail-biting matches that have helped to mould the Club throughout its long history.

With a fitting Foreword by legendary Watford Manager, Graham Taylor OBE, this book will provide hours of entertainment for the whole family who, whilst licking their wounds, can console themselves in the knowledge that £1 from the sale of each copy will be donated to the charity Sense, which helps deaf and blind people of all ages lead fuller and happier lives.

OTHER BOOKS BY CHRIS COWLIN:

The Official Colchester United Quiz Book

Foreword by: Karl Duguid

ISBN: 1-904444-88-1   978-1904444-88-6

Price: £5.99

Question: How many U's are there in Colchester? Answer: One, of course - as all Colchester United fans ought to know. And, if that little teaser caught you out, then brace yourselves for 750 more tricky questions, relating to your favourite team, the U's.

Covering all aspects of the club, from players and managers to nationalities and every conceivable tournament, you will be required to U's your brainpower to its limit to come up with all the answers and amaze (or otherwise) your friends and family with the depth of your knowledge about the club.

With a fitting Foreword by Karl Duguid, this book will trigger recollections of favourite players past and present, nail-biting matches, and all the club's highs and lows over their long history. A veritable treasure trove of facts and figures is at your fingertips – enjoy!

The Official Norwich City Quiz Book

Foreword by: Bryan Gunn

ISBN: 1-904444-80-6   978-1-904444-80-0

Price: £7.99

Will you be singing like a Canary as you fly with ease through this book's 1,000 challenging quiz questions about Norwich City Football Club, or will you have flown the Nest too soon and come crashing to the ground spitting feathers?

Covering all aspects of the club's history, including top goalscorers, transfers, managers, Cup competitions, League positions, awards, legendary players and nationalities, it will push to the limit even the most ardent aficionados' knowledge of their favourite team.

With a fitting foreword by the legendary Bryan Gunn, this book is guaranteed to trigger fond recollections of all the nail-biting matches and colourful characters that have shaped the club over the years, as well as providing a wealth of interesting facts and figures with which to impress your friends and family.

OTHER BOOKS BY CHRIS COWLIN:

The Official Leicester City Quiz Book
Foreword by: Tony Cottee
ISBN: 1-904444-86-5   978-1904444-86-2
Price: £7.99
Can you outfox your friends and family by answering the 1,000 cunning questions about Leicester City Football Club contained in this quiz book, or will you be like a rabbit caught in the headlights?
Questions cover all aspects of the club, from memorable managers and players to transfer fees, opponents and awards, and are sure to conjure up fond reminiscences of the colourful characters and nail-biting matches that have peppered the club's long history.
With a fitting foreword by Tony Cottee, this is as much a treasure trove of interesting facts and figures as it is a quiz book, and is guaranteed to provide hours of entertainment for young and old alike.

The British TV Sitcom Quiz Book
Foreword by: Brian Murphy
ISBN: 1-906358-20-6   978-1-906358-20-4
Price: £7.99
Television situation comedy classics have issued forth from the pens of genius writers and partnerships unabated for the last 50 years in Britain and, if you think you know all there is to know as an aficionado, you may find yourself laughing on the other side of your face as you attempt to conjure up the answers to the 1,000 testing quiz questions contained in this book.
All aspects of the genre are covered – the many series, the creators, the unforgettable, larger-than-life characters, and the wonderful actors and actresses that have made them come to life in comedies ranging from Hancock's Half Hour in the 1950s, through the innumerable greats that have graced every subsequent decade of the last century, to The Office of the new millennium – so even the most ardent sitcom fans will need their wits about them.
This book is as much a treasure trove of fascinating facts and figures as it is an entertaining quiz book for all the family, and it is sure to sort out the Victor Meldrews from the David Brents, stir up many fond memories, create plenty of smiles and oil a few chuckle muscles along the way.

special days for seriously ill young adults

ABOUT
WILLOW FOUNDATION

Special days aim to provide young adults living with life-threatening conditions a chance to escape the pressures of their daily routine and share quality time with family and/or friends.

Every special day is of the young person's choosing - it could involve fulfilling a lifelong dream or it could simply offer an opportunity to bring some much needed normality back into their lives.

The Foundation will endeavour to fulfil the special day request however imaginative and, if possible, exceed expectations.

To date the charity has organised and funded special days for young adults living with a wide range of serious conditions including amongst others; cancer, motor neurone disease, cystic fibrosis, organ failure, multiple sclerosis (later stages) and heart disease.

Bob & Megs Wilson founded the Willow Foundation in memory of their daughter, Anna who died of cancer aged 31.

For more information please contact:
Willow Foundation, Willow House, 18 Salisbury Square,
Hatfield, Hertfordshire, AL9 5BE
Tel: 01707 259777   Fax: 01707 259289
or email: info@willowfoundation.org.uk

REVIEWS

"If you, like me, love to test your knowledge in a good football quiz, then this book is must. Great questions about our beloved Hammers." - **www.westham.no**

"Ideal for the journey to the match, a get together in the pub, or even just to impress the family, the West Ham Quiz Book is a must for all Irons, everywhere. Enjoy!"
- www.footballheaven.net

"This is the sort of book I can give as a present to people. The questions are well thought out, Chris Cowlin must have done an awful lot of research. I'm very impressed!"
www.franklampard.net

"This is a brilliant quiz book."
- Mike Hallowell, The Sheilds Gazette

"A terrific test of all things Hammers related... A must have for every West Ham fan!"
- Geoff Hillyer, SGR Colchester 96.1 FM

"Sends you on a wonderful trip down memory lane!"
www.bobbymooreonline.co.uk

"The book is a must for all West Ham fans."
- www.a2zsoccer.com

"An absolute must for any West Ham fan who enjoys testing their knowledge of the Hammers!"
- www.sporting-heroes.net

REVIEWS

*"There are also a lot of questions aimed at more recent additions to the supporters ranks so this book is a great read no matter how old you are." - **The Ironworks Gazette**

*"Covering every aspect of the team's history, such as players, managers, opponents, transfers, nationalities and every competition." - **Shoot Magazine**

*"How much do you think you know about the Hammers? If you want to find out if you are a West Ham United expert then get the new West Ham Quiz Book" - **Hammers Official Programme**

"No question about it, all Hammers fans should enjoy this!" **Ex-Magazine** (Retro Magazine dedicated to former players of West Ham United)

*"If you're born to be Claret and Blue, this is the Christmas stocking filler for you!" - **www.westhamfans.org**

*"An absolute must for all die hard Hammers, like myself. Perfect pre-match entertainment with a pint and a pie, also doubling up as a great source of reference on West Ham United." - **Perry Fenwick**

*"I found the book very entertaining and a must for all West Ham supporters. I did answer some of the questions as I had the good fortune of referring at Upton Park." - **Ray Lewis**

REVIEWS

"It looks a great read! I am even trying it out on Sir Geoff Hurst!" **- Dave Davies**

"The quiz book is absolutely superb. The range of questions, spanning so many decades is interesting and at times extremely informative!" **- Scott Duxbury**

"A very comprensive quiz book that will be of great interest to all Hammers fans - and help to keep them entertained." **- Peter Stewart**

"A well balanced mixture of fun and formidable questions that will put even the most ardent Hammers fan to the test! A great book to have on your shelf pre or post match!" **- Michael Goodwin, Time FM 107.5**

"A quiz book for all ages, a must for any Hammers fan!" **- John Motson**

"A book for anoraks, aficionados or serious students of West Hamology – you decide. Once you get started you are sure to get hooked. Enjoy!" **- Kriss Akabusi**

"A book that every Hammers fan will not be able to put down. I have watched West Ham for half a centery and the questions brought back amazing memories from John Lyall at left back onwards. Well done Chris." **- Richard Digance**

REVIEWS

"Great book for the ardent Hammers fan!
We can relive all the highs!" - **Graham Gooch**

"A lot of fun - a must for West Ham fans. Well done Chris."
- **Terence Stamp**

"A must for all Irons fans!" - **Tommy Walsh**

"I'd fight Julian Dicks to get my hands on a copy.
It made me a very happy Hammer." - **Paul Ross**

"West Ham United has a great history and tradition. A quiz
book that covers the whole spectrum of West Ham life - a
fantastic read!" - **Mark Ward**

"Well set out, not to hard which will give the younger fans a
chance to enjoy the book as well as the older ones.
Well done Chris." - **Glenn Roeder**

"A must for all West Ham fans, especially on those long away
trips! Good variety, a few teasers and interesting too!"
- **Tony Carr**

"A must for all Hammers fans, young and old, full
of interesting facts and memories." - **Peter Grant**

"This is the sort of book that will settle a few arguments -
and probably start a few more! An ideal present (stocking
filler?) for the Statto Hammer!" - **www.kumb.com**

"A book that will entertain any West Ham United fan,
it certainly entertained the Boys of 86 squad!"
- **www.boysof86events.co.uk**